FEEDING
THE SOUL

(because it's my business)

FINDING OUR WAY TO JOY, LOVE, AND FREEDOM

WM

WILLIAM MORROW
An Imprint of HarperCollins*Publishers*

FEEDING
THE SOUL

(because it's my business)

TABITHA BROWN

HarperCollins books may be purchased for educational, business, or sales promotional use. For information, please email the Special Markets Department at SPsales@harpercollins.com.

FIRST EDITION

Designed by Bonni Leon-Berman

Library of Congress Cataloging-in-Publication Data has been applied for.

ISBN 978-0-06-308028-7

21 22 23 24 25   LSC   10 9 8 7 6 5 4 3 2 1

TO MOMA AND DADDY:

Thank you for giving me life and
for always encouraging me to be me!

CONTENTS

A NOTE FROM TAB

Be sure to keep your eyes open for my popular TSAs—Tabitha Service Announcements—and some of my favorite easy vegan recipes from my YouTube and TikTok channels.

But look here, honey. I know you'll be looking for measurements and things. And if I have them, I'll give them to you. But in Tab's kitchen, we cook by the spirit. Like I always say, if you need an exact recipe every time you cook, you don't trust yourself. Let's trust ourselves, and however much you are moved to use, that's what you use.

Recipes in This Book

INTRODUCTION

HELLO THERE

Honey, how y'all doing? Y'all alright? Trying to hang in there?

Listen, I understand. I really do. And because we all have either gone through something, are currently going through something, or are *about* to go through something, I thought I'd share my heart and story with you. The elders in the church of my childhood back in Eden and Ruffin, North Carolina, used to sing a song called "How I Got Over." It was a declaration of not just the faithfulness of God but their own persistence through both good and hard times. It was a signpost that pointed directly to the ways they chose to live and love in order to make it to a point where they could say, "Hey, y'all, I'm good. I made it to the good part." In a way, this book is my "How I Got Over" declaration to you. It is filled with both affirmations and inspiration on how to live your life with an abundance of love, joy, peace of mind, and freedom.

You like that?

Very good.

It's such a powerful thing to rise out of the depths of darkness. Ask me how I know! There's an old saying I used to hear from my mom. When asked how she was doing, she would respond, "Ooh, I thank God I don't look like what I've been through." Isn't that the truth? I know some people will say, "Oh, Tab, your life is amazing!" Well, that's because they are only looking on the outside. They are only seeing the fruit instead of the roots. Honey, remember, the same day we plant our seeds is not the same day we eat the fruit. It takes time before the harvest comes. Sure, today I don't look like depression. I don't look like anxiety or migraines or autoimmune illness. I don't look like any of those things, but guess what? I've been through them all. There was a time when I didn't think I would ever make it out of a very lost and dark place.

But I did.

And when I received my breakthrough, I made a sincere promise to God that because He brought me out of the darkness, I would always try to be a light for others to follow suit.

So, honey, I'm writing this book to bring you some light. I want you to know that you are loved. That you are not alone, despite what the journey might look like right now for you. More than anything I want to inspire you to be your best self, and maybe even make you laugh a little bit along the way. If you happen to cry a little, too, that's your business. The world is tough right now. There's enough sorrow and frustration to go around. More people are struggling with depression and anxiety than ever before. The fear of the unknown has caused so much stress and fear. But know this: Whatever it is you are feeling right now, whatever you may be going through, it *will* pass.

I won't lie to you. It probably won't happen overnight. It may not end tomorrow or even the next day. But I'm a living witness to the fact that life will not always be hard.

There was a time in my life when I just knew I had it all. In the new year of 2008, I made a vision board and posted images and messages like *Working Actress in 2008* and *Brand-new Mercedes* on it. I'd taken my headshots, and, baby, I was ready! And that year I worked like never before. I starred in several independent films and bought a house and a Mercedes. In my mind, I was living the dream. *This vision board thing is wonderful,* I thought.

But then, in 2009, a proverbial storm came tearing through my life and uprooting my dream. I couldn't book a single job as an actress. My dream car was constantly breaking down. The house we'd just bought in the desert was causing us more harm than good. It was too far away from LA. Too far from the village we'd created in our first five years of living there. We'd created such an amazing circle of friends who became our family, our village, but we were so far away from them that no one could ever come to see us. Everyone came for the housewarming, but we went from people coming over every Sunday for dinner to a few friends coming once or twice a year.

I was miserable and feeling so lost. But then, I heard in my spirit a lesson I will never forget: "Be specific, Tabitha. You asked for things and you were blessed with them. But you didn't specify the details." See, honey, I'd prayed for a house, but I didn't pray about where that house should be. I'd prayed for a car, but I didn't pray about affordability or getting one in good condition. The lesson? Be careful what you ask for; you just may get it. And when you do get it, are you truly prepared to maintain and keep the very things you requested? Be careful about praying for more without praying that you are ready for it when *more* comes!

I also figured out that while storms will inevitably come, we must maintain our hope for a better tomorrow. We must be willing to refine our asks and learn the lessons these storms are sent to teach us. Nowadays my prayers look a little different. I say, "Lord, prepare me for what it is I think I want. Prepare me for the blessings, so I will know how to keep them when I get them. And Lord, sustain me through the storm with hope, faith, and joy."

This book is my gift to you. It is a gift of love and light so that you will not just survive what you're going through, but thrive in the midst of it. I want you to experience true joy as you read these stories from my life. Because, honey, who doesn't need joy? Who doesn't need hope? Hope is the ultimate driver of our faith. It's the very thing that helps so many of us get through our day. Faith allows us to believe that things will get better. It pushes us to keep going even when everything else says, *Give up!*

I believe the words of civil rights activist Ella Baker, who once said, "Give light and people will find the way." That's what I mean by *feeding the soul*. My prayer is that every story, recipe, and TSA (Tabitha Service Announcement) will get you that much closer to reclaiming your hope and restoring your faith. Feeding your soul with all this joy helps feed me at the same time, honey. Laugh and cry, a little or a lot (whichever, because that's your business). The goal is for you to know that you are seen, loved, and heard.

Then you can turn right around and pass that same love and joy along to someone else.

When you turn the last page of this book, I want you to know, without any doubt, that you can go on. Those country church elders would probably say something like, "Run on and see what the end's gon' be." That's it! No matter what things may look like right now, no matter your circumstance, keep going, honey. And while you're on that journey, I want you to know that you are never alone. I want to draw you into my arms with my words and wrap them around you in a big ol' Auntie Tab hug. I want the numbness to finally melt away, and for you to feel all of who God created you to be!

It's time to get back to you. To discover your true self, maybe even for the first time. To allow those parts of ourselves that have been hidden to be released and shine. It's time we all get back to understanding ourselves. To connect again to what makes us come alive. Let's climb new heights together and gain new insight on ourselves, our relationships, our careers, and anything else we dream of improving.

It's way too easy to get stuck nowadays. We are overwhelmed with information, but aren't often given the chance to build our empathy muscles so we can use that information wisely and to our benefit. Empathy, or the lack thereof, plays a huge part in the way we engage each other. In the age of social media, it's so easy to be overwhelmed by the noise of these platforms if you're not careful. It's also easy to allow that noise to turn you into someone you are not. What I've come to learn is that everyone, no matter what they post, has their own battles. Sometimes people post messages of hate, anger, or just nastiness, and that likely means that person is hurting. No, it doesn't make them right. But it definitely makes them hurt. And when people are hurting, they often want to inflict that same pain on others. But here's the real catch: If you don't have empathy, you might be quick to respond to that person with the same energy they're giving. Then it becomes a never-ending circle of toxic communication.

Tapping into our ability to empathize means understanding just how hurt a person must be, how deep their pain must go, in order to spew hate out into the world. When I have experienced that kind of hatred, I have to stop and think about how hurt this person must be, and I often wonder if something tragic happened to them if they're choosing to live their life that way. I'm human, so of course there are times when I may want to lash back. But I also know that returning negative energy to someone who is already sitting deep in it won't change them or me. It will only put more negative energy into the world. And honey, I only want to be responsible for putting love into the world. So when hate comes my way, I try to sit back for a minute. I don't ever respond immediately. It's important for me to take the time to think about why someone is doing what they're doing. That way, I can respond, if I choose to, from a place of love. Love really is at the root of empathy.

Empathy also shows up in the way we respond to people

who find themselves sharing the hard things going on in their lives. It takes a lot of vulnerability, honey, to put yourself out there and talk about the not-so-great situations in one's life. When this happens, some people are inclined to react by saying things like, "Oh, they just want attention." And the truth is, maybe they do! Maybe that's what they've been lacking in their lives. Maybe no one has paid attention to them. Maybe no one has spoken to them in years, and the internet is their only outlet to get feedback of any sort, to get some form of recognition that they are still alive. But only when we have a posture of empathy are we really able to come at it from that perspective. Only empathy will make you say, "Let me really look at this person's comment. Let me really take some time to send them a message and say, 'You know what? I see you. I hear what you're saying, and I love you.'" If we don't have empathy, then we certainly won't have the patience for that kind of compassionate response. Oh, but if we do have empathy? Honey, we could truly change somebody's life and world. I honestly believe that.

For some folks, it will take time to strengthen the capacity for empathy; to be able to hold space for someone. And unfortunately, sometimes we have to go through something major in our own lives to understand that life is often bigger and more complicated than what is on the surface. That's usually when we'll feel for people, because we've felt the sting of loneliness or longing or whatever is at the root of their pain. We finally understand that every day doesn't feel so great, and there are days that any of us might wish we could have a hug or someone to tell us, "It's going to be alright." When that empathy muscle is developed, we just might find ourselves being that person for someone else. That's also how love spreads.

No matter what, though, we don't have to stay in a stuck place. We can dream better dreams and empower ourselves to move forward with love and grace. When you close this book, I need you to be able to say, "You know what? Yes, I can! Yes, I will! Yes, I am!" You'll be excited about taking some chances. Excited about not feeling stuck. You will know that you can absolutely take charge over your life and feel good about it.

I'm often asked what I mean when I say, "Because it's my business." Well, honey, it means exactly what it says. My life is my business. Your life is your business. If we all would just shift our focus to making sure we are developing our own character, taking care of our own families, and loving on our own communities, then without doubt we would see a shift in the way our world operates. If you are so busy trying to mind everybody else's business—by being judgmental and negative; by tearing someone down because of jealousy, differences, or fear—then, baby, you will eventually go *out* of business. I don't want that for anyone.

Focus on *your* life, honey. Do whatever it is that pleases you. Put yourself first. Fill your own cup so you'll have enough to share when it comes time to pour out those amazing gifts of yours. Do things that make you happy. I know what social media tells us, but take it from someone who is considered an influencer: It really doesn't matter what other people think. You will be the most successful when you choose to be the most authentic. When you mind your business, more business will come. Don't be ashamed of living your life to the fullest. Don't let fear keep you bound to an identity that was never yours. Walk into your freedom with your head held high!

And I suppose that's really the bottom line. This book is my way of modeling freedom through testimony. I've been through some things. But one day I decided I would no longer be bound by the residue of my past. I decided that I would no longer allow what so-and-so said to define me. I chose freedom. Freedom to be. Freedom to trust. Freedom to be able to say "Because it's my business" and really mean it. And that, honey, is what I want most for you.

To get free and stay free, and never apologize for it.

I love you,
Tab

Part One

THAT'S
YOUR
BUSINESS

YOUR GIFTS,
YOUR BUSINESS

"We are all gifted. That is our inheritance."

—ETHEL WATERS

I have a question for you, honey. One that maybe you haven't been asked in a good while, if at all. What gifts were you born with that you are not using? What are those things that you can say without a shadow of a doubt, "I'm gifted in this area. This comes naturally for me"? Some people are great at math. Others are great at teaching children. Some folks can sing the paint off the walls, and others can draw anything with scary accuracy. So I ask you again: What gifts do you have that you're not using?

Listen, we were born with gifts, talents, and abilities in

order to use them. Not to let them stay dormant inside of us. Not to be silent about them. Not to carry them right on to the grave without doing a thing about them. There's an old adage that says, "The richest place in the world is the cemetery." Too many people leave this world without ever letting their brilliance and creativity see the light of day.

Don't you dare be one of them! Start using those gifts— and watch your world start to change.

Growing up, I had so many moments that really scared me when it came to recognizing the gifts I had and trying to figure out what to do with them. My whole life, I've always been funny. Even as a child, I knew I could make people laugh. I used to be the joke teller at all the cookouts when I was a kid. I loved jokes and laughter so much, my daddy bought me my first joke book when I was in third grade. Oh, God, how I loved those books! I would read them all the time, and even came up with my own jokes that I'd test out on the family. I couldn't wait for the next big family gathering so I could share my latest jokes or performance. My family would laugh until they cried sometimes. It made me feel so good to know I was giving them so much joy. I didn't realize that my sense of humor and timing were actual divine gifts until, of course, much later in life.

But there was another gift. One that, for a while there, I wouldn't talk about. I was sure that people wouldn't understand it, or they would be so frightened by it that they'd think I was crazy and stay away from me altogether. I have the gift of seeing and dreaming. Some folks back home call it "second sight."

I had many dreams as a child—about various relatives or certain circumstances—that felt like premonitions. One night, when I was six or seven years old, I had a dream that I was stuck in the automatic sliding doors at the grocery store. I saw myself, my arms and legs flailing, trying to escape the opening and closing of the door on my body. When I woke up, I told my mama and she comforted me. Later that week, I was with my neighbor when she stopped at the grocery for a few things. Honey, lo and behold, the doors closed right in on me just like in my dream. I'd dreamed about it, and it had come to pass.

It was so strange at first, to continuously receive these visions. But then it just became my norm. I finally said to myself, *Oh, wait, this is a gift I have. I dream things and they happen.* It became a real thing for me. As I got older, I would talk about my dreams often, and my mama would affirm that she'd always known I had the gift.

But this isn't something that's easy to share with people. There's this fear of people saying, "Oh, she's crazy!" If I were to always tell people what I saw about their lives, they'd probably slowly back away from me, their faces revealing their skepticism. But there also comes a point in your life when, in order to be authentic, you have to embrace all of what makes you who you are. As I came into adulthood, this gift of mine was something I couldn't ignore, even when I desperately wanted to. I can't control the visions or the dreams; they just happen.

My husband, Chance, and I first moved to Los Angeles in 2004, and honey, there wasn't a silver spoon in sight. We lived in an apartment complex in Baldwin Hills near Don Tomaso Drive that required us to take fifty-one stairs—yes, I counted—to our front door. We had a neighbor named Kim who seemed very sweet, although we didn't know her very well. She had the cutest baby boy named Devon, and as time went on, we did the typical friendly neighbor thing. We'd speak and say, "Hey, how are you?" when we passed each other, but didn't get too involved in each other's lives. But there was something in my spirit that pressed me to try for more.

I felt led to invite her over one day with another friend. While Kim was there, she said, "I have to go to this little birthday dinner later. Do you guys want to go with me? You can ride with me." I said, "Sure." I hadn't really been out in LA yet, so I thought, *Oh, this will be interesting. A little fun something to do.*

But as we were leaving, it happened. We were going down those forever stairs and Kim was holding Devon, who was about one at the time. As she placed him on her hip, I got a mental image of a coffin with a man in it. Somehow, I instantly knew that it was this little boy's father. I have no idea how I knew, and I certainly didn't know where the image came from or why it came to me, but there it was. As soon as I saw it, I thought, *Oh my God, this baby's father has passed away.*

As Kim was putting Devon into the car seat, she said, "I need to take my son to my mom's house before we go." Her next words nearly knocked the breath out of me.

"It's just been so hard because his dad isn't with me. I lost his dad when I was pregnant."

I almost passed out.

Wait a minute. What just happened?

I honestly didn't know what to say. There was no way I could admit, "Yeah, I knew that." She wouldn't have believed me anyway. But that experience was the beginning of me truly accepting that the gift was not only real, but something that would always be a part of my life. The dreams and visions I'd always had were undeniable. But again, how do you share something like that with someone?

Well, maybe God is trying to teach me something here. I don't know, I thought.

That was an understatement.

A couple of months later, Kim and I took Devon and my daughter Choyce to the fair. It was in Orange County, a bit of a drive away from where we lived. On our way back, I volunteered to drive Kim's Lincoln Navigator, since she'd driven us there.

"Okay. That's great," she said.

As I was getting on the freeway, it happened again. I saw the most terrible image in my mind. I saw my three-year-old daughter opening the door and falling onto the freeway. I literally saw her rolling down the concrete as cars rushed past. It was the scariest vision I'd ever seen. This wasn't the time to be quiet like before.

Okay, I've got to say something.

"Do your doors lock automatically? Are the doors in the

back locked? Are the doors around the kids locked?" I asked.

"Yeah, yeah. They lock automatically. Why?" she said.

"I don't know. I just had this very weird thing happen."

I didn't go into detail, but not even two minutes later, we heard the whooshing of wind coming from the back seat. Despite being strapped in, Choyce had opened the back door.

"Lord have . . ." Honey, my heart was racing so fast. I *knew* it was going to happen. I had already seen it. Even though Kim told me the doors were locked, my daughter had figured out how to get hers open. While doing seventy-five miles per hour on the freeway, I swung and swerved the door so the door would slam back shut. Then I pulled over. My whole body was shaking. Kim was staring wide-eyed at me. "You knew that was going to happen! How did you know that was going to happen?!"

"I don't know, honey, but I saw it," I said.

After calming myself down and soothing Choyce, I got back on the road. From that day on, I chose to listen to my spirit. Though I was still very much afraid of these dreams and visions, I knew my life was calling me to embrace them. Embracing my gift would empower it.

When my mother was sick and in her final days, we had so many wonderful conversations. We'd sit together and talk for hours about so many things. I'll never forget one night when she asked me, "Are you ready to talk?"

"What are you talking about, Moma?"

"Are you ready to talk?" she asked me again.

She knew. These visions I would see and these dreams I would have, they were getting stronger and stronger. But, of course, I played like I didn't know what she was asking.

"Talk about what?"

"The things that you're seeing."

The tone of her voice was measured, even as it was filled with love.

"I told you as a little girl that you have the gift of dreaming," she continued. "But you also have the gift of seeing. God has chosen you for things that He can trust you with. You need a mentor." My mother recognized the gift in me because she had it herself. But she also knew she was on her way out of this world and would not be there to help me navigate using it.

In her own way, she was saying, "Don't be afraid of it. God has trusted you with this gift."

And if I'm honest, there was a season in my life when I didn't want the gift at all. I didn't want people to think I was nuts. I'd spoken with a pastor who I was told could help me make sense of it all, but I'd begun to see some things about his life and confirm they were true, which, I suppose, scared him. He stopped talking to me. Just stopped engaging altogether. This not only made me sad, it made me never want to share with anyone else. After that, my prayer was clearer than ever: "Oh, God, please take this away from me. I don't want it anymore."

For a couple of years, I thought my gift had disappeared. I didn't have visions or special dreams for a while. But you know what? I kind of missed it—I felt like I wasn't complete. There definitely seemed to be a trade-off.

When I fell ill in 2016, the dreams and visions became stronger, and I started having intimate conversations with God even more often. And eventually, I freed myself from the stigma of it all. I now welcome the visions. I welcome the dreams. I'm so thankful and far from afraid when God gives me messages to share with people. I surrendered and accepted my gift and assignment.

And that's just it. We have to embrace the gifts that God gives us—no matter what they are. You know the saying "If you don't use it, you'll lose it"? It's true, love. And losing it might seem like something you want in the short term, when fear and the need for acceptance overwhelm you, but trust me, losing your gift might also mean losing the purpose attached to it, and you don't want that.

Listen: I could have chosen not to share my gift of supernatural sight with you out of fear that some readers might feel uncomfortable. I certainly could have not put it in the very first chapter. But here's the thing: We all have something we've been given that ultimately will serve and fulfill our life's purpose. You might not be able to make people laugh or have dreams and visions, but I promise you, honey, there is something beautiful within you. Do the work to uncover it. No matter what people might say or think about it, seize that gift. Then watch how it blesses you and everyone you encounter. I'm introducing you to this part of me because I know for sure that the very first lesson to living and loving well is trusting the gifts God has given you. To believe in them so much that you move through life with an agency and intention that is solely yours. Your gifts, love, are 100 percent your business.

TSA

 Recently, as I prepared to celebrate my forty-second birthday, I realized that my dreams to become a performer and help people through my art were just now coming true. In fact, it's just been in the last year that my whole entire life has changed. This affirmed for me that we are never too young or too old to start dreaming. And more than that, we're never too old for our dreams to come true. I don't care what you've done. I don't care how many mistakes you've made. I don't care how many times you've failed. I don't care how many nos you've received. You're still worthy, and that means your dreams can still come true. They can still happen. If you keep going, if you keep believing, they're yours.

Don't believe the lie that you can't have the desires of your heart. God said we can. But the only way we can have it is if we believe we can. Too many times, we convince ourselves that either we've done something so bad that we don't deserve what we dream of, or we've made one too many bad choices and our circumstances won't allow us to see our dreams come true. Baby, that is not true. It just isn't. You can still have the desires of your heart. Don't you dare talk yourself out of your dreams.

And here's another thing: If you think your dream is too big, it's actually probably too small. Honey, I'm a witness that God will say to our little dreams, "That's it? Girl, you can do that. Let me show you what I can do." But we just have to hold on. Hold on at twenty-five, thirty, forty, fifty, sixty, or seventy. Hold on no matter what. It took me more than twenty years to get here. Twenty-three years of pursuing a career in acting, and God took me on a detour. But honey, the sights He showed me on that detour, I'd never change it. I'm so grateful for those lessons.

My daddy was sixty-five when he opened his own barber shop. His dream was always to open his own shop. His whole life, that was his desire. And at sixty-five, he did exactly that. So I don't care how old you are or how long you've done the same old thing. You can still do something new. You can still have something new. Why? Because God said so. Just believe it, okay? Let God blow your mind.

VEGAN TUNA SALAD (UN-TUNA) WRAP

My mama used to make the best tuna salad. Ooh, it was so good. She used to make that tuna salad, honey, and put them crackers on the side—we were eating good! You couldn't tell us we weren't having a five-course meal. So when I make un-tuna salad, I think of Moma.

Canned chickpeas (garbanzo beans)

Chopped purple (red) onion

Vegan mayo

Yellow mustard

Sweet relish

A little bit of garlic powder

Dill *(fresh or dried, that's your business)*

Furikake

Salt

Fresh lemon juice

Black salt *(optional, not for a salt taste but to give the un-tuna an egglike flavor)*

Tomato or spinach wrap, or lettuce wrap, or crackers

Mixed greens

Tomatoes

Chopped white onion

Drain your chickpeas, put them in a bowl, and use a fork or potato masher to get that tuna-ish consistency.

Then add your onion.

Put the mixture in a blender and pulse to lightly mix. (Make sure it's blended well—no huge chunks—but don't be heavy-handed like I can be sometimes.)

Return the mixture to your bowl.

Throw some relish in there.

Then the mayo.

Just a little mustard *(unless you like it, then that's your business)*.

Add the dill, garlic powder, and furikake.

A little salt.

A squirt of lemon.

Finally, if you have it, add just a little bit of your black salt.

Now just stir it up. Make sure you get everything evenly distributed, okay?

Eat it with crackers or in your wrap like I do, with all the extra fixins.

Get into it, honey. I promise you it's not tuna. Just a little something better.

YOU HAVE
TO FIX
IT FIRST

"Dreams do not come true just because you dream them. It's hard work that makes things happen. It's hard work that creates change."

—SHONDA RHIMES

I love you all so much that I'd be totally remiss if I didn't say the hard things. Here's a hard thing: Taking owner-ship of your life might just mean you have to stop saying, "Oh, *fix it,* Jesus!" when you know you are going to keep do-ing the same things that are breaking it. Too many of us are praying for healing but still eating the same things that are making us sick. We keep asking God to heal us from lung cancer, but are we still smoking cigarettes? We're desperate to lower our cholesterol levels, but are we still eating all the fatty meats? How does that work, honey? We've all by now heard one definition of insanity: doing the same thing over and over again and expecting different results. The bottom line is this: Whatever changes we long for in our lives, we have to do our part.

And yes, I hear you out there. "Tab, what I eat or smoke is my business."

It is, baby. It really is. And please know that I'm not judging you one bit. But I do love you enough to suggest that if you choose to still do those things, you have to right-size your expectations of divine intervention when the outcomes align with your choices and not your heart's desires.

When I was finally able to make it to Los Angeles in pursuit of my acting dreams, I just knew that something or somebody was going to be waiting on me when I got into town. I'd heard God clearly, and my spirit had been awakened in a way that propelled me all the way from Greensboro, North Carolina, to LA. But guess what I learned mighty quickly when I got here?

Nobody was waiting for me.

I literally had to start from the bottom. From scratch. But I knew I had this dream. I had goals. I wanted to be in entertainment, to be an actress. And I suppose I could have sat in my apartment wanting and desiring but never actually doing what needed to be done to get where I wanted to go. So while I didn't know anyone and didn't know much at all about the business, honey, I did know what I'd been taught long ago by my mother and father: Faith without works is dead. I had the faith that I could one day become a working entertainer, but I also had to do the work. God put this dream in my heart at a very early age, but He didn't just put it there for me to sit on it. God said, "Listen, if you go ahead and do what you need to do, I will do my part."

What I "needed to do" was act. It was—and is—my passion. It's like breathing for me. When I don't do it, if I go too long without performing, it's like my air is cut off—so much so that I start to not feel well. I think I have such a strong connection to acting because I see it as my opportunity to disappear. I get to become someone else. I often get to do things I wouldn't be able to do in my regular life, like play someone mentally ill and/or be very mean. I get to be the doctor or the lawyer; prostitute or drug addict. I just get to explore the minds and hearts of the characters I bring to life, and it helps me understand myself and others better.

But most important, I get to tell the stories of people who might not otherwise have a voice. Everybody has a story to tell, no matter where they're from, what they've done—good or bad—or what they do. So to be able to embody those lived experiences and create them on the screen gives me life. And truthfully, breathing life into a character is just so much fun. It never feels like work.

I suppose there's also the feeling I get when I see people enjoying themselves because of my work. Making Moma and Daddy laugh at cookouts with my little joke book was so rewarding. It felt so good. And then growing up and doing theater in school and performing in community theater, there was something fulfilling in hearing people gasp for air when I did something onstage. When they'd laugh out loud or sit with tears streaming down their faces from my performance, it was such an affirmation of the gift God had given me.

So I began to study. I was in acting class for years. I will still take an acting class today, honey, because that's my business. I auditioned for all kinds of roles and took some that didn't even pay, just for the experience. I took many acting workshops and continuously honed my craft. Yes, I wanted that big opportunity. I was waiting for it. But you know what else I was doing while I was waiting? I was working. God certainly controls everything, but I honestly believe that He honors us for doing our part. He is looking for our commitment and investment in that thing we feel called to do.

I'm a living, breathing witness to this, honey. Yes, I prayed. I created vision boards and wrote extensive plans in my journals. But I also woke up every day and worked toward those things I envisioned.

I've been on so many sets, and it always blows me away that I get to do what I do. I show up wanting nothing in return other than to do my job and to do it well. But then a director, producer, or cast member says something like, "Oh my God, that was amazing," and it just snaps me into the reality of this gift. All I can say in that moment is, "Oh wow, thank you."

I remember when I had a role on an episode of *Will &*

Grace. With the exception of an independent film I'd done that year, this was my first acting job in the couple of years since I'd returned to auditioning. I hadn't really been on a studio lot. I was so nervous, but also excited. It was also my first time in front of a live studio audience, so that immediately took me back to doing theater and being able to hear the audience laugh. That role really gave me new life, a new purpose. It inspired me to want to do more. I thought, *People need this. People need to laugh.*

I remember sitting in that studio after we wrapped, having hit my lines every time and heard how the crowd just organically laughed. My heart was full. At the end of a taping, they do a curtain call where they introduce the cast. Everyone comes out and takes their bow. When they called my name, the audience cheered. They remembered me. I thought, *Things can't get any better.* I suppose God said, "Watch me." At the end of the taping, Max Mutchnick, the creator of *Will & Grace,* walked up to me, shook my hand, and said, "Wow. You are such a professional. You're so funny, and you really made the show tonight." That was huge for me. It blew my mind.

But honey, God wasn't done yet.

Fast-forward a year later, and now Max Mutchnick and I are developing my own show for ABC. A seed that day—me, as an actor—was unknowingly planted, and now it has come back around in full bloom. He remembered me, reached out, and said, "What else do you want to do?" I said, "Well, I do have this show idea. I want to be known as America's mom. I want to tell funny stories that are relatable from the point of view of a woman, mother, and dreamer. I want to speak to the person who is struggling to keep it together while not losing herself in the process." And I knew it had to be a comedy. *People need to laugh.*

He loved the idea and said *yes.* And then I said *yes.* And then we got the deal at ABC.

Even when I tried to run from acting, tried to give up on it because I thought I didn't deserve it, God saw fit to make sure I couldn't stop. God made sure to always remind me that He had a plan for me. So I kept going.

And I'm so glad I did. Acting is everything to me.

I once produced a short film about my mother and asked my sister, who was not an actress at all, to star in it. I said, "You look exactly like Moma. You think you could play Moma in my little short film?" And without any hesitation, she said yes. She played our mother during her illness, particularly the time period when she was on a ventilator. I remember walking back into the room after my sister was set up on the hospital bed and breaking completely down. She cried, too. All I saw was my mama. My sister literally brought my mama back to me for a minute. We imitated life. We told a story and we weren't afraid. That's the power of acting.

Acting gives you the power to explore myriad emotions and to use that ability to create beautiful art. In that moment with my sister, acting gave us the freedom to cry and grieve; to remember the good times, but most important, to help those who watched the film grieve and find a little bit of light in their own situation.

Now, after some good years and some not-so-good ones, all the things I worked toward have come to pass. And as you might have guessed, the outcomes are even bigger than I could have ever imagined. But that was *after* I set my hand to the plow and worked to nurture those seeds He planted long ago. I did my best, then God did the rest. Ohh, God, I thank you!

So what are you really saying, Tab?

As an actress, influencer, and motivational speaker, I'm clear that none of these titles, none of these opportunities came about because I said, "Oh, God will bring it to me." It was because I believed God had something more for me and I just kept working until He said, "Yes, now it's time." And I continue to do that, because even though things are great now, I know there is still more to come.

Of course, there is something bigger out there working on our behalf. I call it God, but you might call it Spirit, Higher Power, Universe, or something else entirely. But believing in that "something" doesn't absolve you from the mighty work you have to do yourself. We must be responsible for our decisions. We must be willing to unpack our heart's desires and then act accordingly. Want to be healthier? Great! Treat your body as the prize possession that it is.

Oh, and stop telling everybody what you *would* have done if you didn't have this or that.

Man, if I didn't have kids...

If I didn't have these bills...

If I lived there...

No, honey. Stop talking about what you could have, would

have, or should have done and just go on out and do it. Stop talking about your past and do what you need to do to move toward the future. I believe in you. Your future is bright. Just walk into the light, baby.

Every new year, we all make our resolutions. We say, "I'm going to start my savings account" or "I'm going to start that business" or "I'm going to work hard to lose or gain weight." Honey, what are you waiting for? Why wait until the New Year or the start of a new week to do what you've wanted to do all year? Yes, energy can shift and you could all of a sudden become motivated on Monday or January first, but let's be honest with ourselves. If you don't have the traits and willpower you need to start today, then how much difference is waiting until the new year going to make? Cultivate your commitment. Examine your motivations. Put yourself first! Develop your self-compassion. Then let all those things be what drives your action so you can sustain it over the long term. Remember, faith without works is dead. Decide today to get to work. Let tomorrow or January first take care of itself. Today is all you know you have for sure anyway, love. And today is as good a day as any to begin taking care of your business.

TSA

 We often drive our lives like we drive our cars. Some folks love to go fast. Others take their time and check out the scenery. All of that is fine. But what I don't understand is letting other folks drive your car. Sure, as children, our parents are in the driver's seat. They guide us along the way until we are mature enough to take the wheel. The same goes for teachers and mentors, to a certain extent. But honey, some of y'all let folks drive your car who shouldn't have even been allowed to ride in it. But there you are, handing over the keys to your mind, heart, and soul. Some people you let drive your car too long. They aren't doing any maintenance on it. Haven't contributed a gallon of gas, but they are still driving your life instead of you. Honey, time's up. It's time to take your keys to your car and your life back. You are the only driver.

3

EVERYONE CAN'T GO

*"You've got to learn to leave the table when
love's no longer being served."*

—NINA SIMONE

One of the things I love about vegan soul food is that it
has the taste of home, of the familiar, but it's actually
good for you. It's the best of both worlds. Sure, you might
prefer the extra butter and everything fried, and that's your
business. I get that. But it's the vegetables that will keep you
healthy and bless your entire life.

The same goes with these word blessings I'm serving. I
know that some of it might not be easy to hear. It challenges
you, maybe even works your nerves a little bit. But it's also
familiar; it's like home. It resonates with that part of you
that wants better for yourself. So you feed your soul with

goodness so you can, as our friend Spock from *Star Trek* says, "Live long and prosper."

So don't get mad at me when I share this next thought with you, okay?

Okay.

Lean in, baby.

Are you leaning?

Are you listening?

Very good.

Here it is:

Everyone can't go with you.

Wait, what?! What do you mean, Tab?

I know people who won't even go to the gym and work out unless they have someone with them. They want a workout partner, which is fine, but if they don't have one, they just don't go to the gym. Why is it okay to sacrifice your fitness goals because you are afraid to enter the building alone? No, honey. That's not the way.

There are going to be parts of your journey that will require you to go it alone. Everyone can't go with you. In fact, I'd argue that there are things that *must* be done on your own or you'll never see the fullness of it. You'll never get it done.

And you might be saying, "Wanting a workout partner isn't a bad thing, Tab." You're right. It isn't. But sometimes we have to look at how we handle the small things to determine how well we'll handle the big ones. Some of the same folks who won't go to the gym to work out by themselves are the same people who haven't started that business they've been thinking about because they're waiting for someone to go in on it with them. There are still others of you who know you should have long ago moved from that town, but you're waiting around hoping somebody will move with you or give you permission. Baby, when are you going to just depend on you? The best bet you'll ever make is the one you make on yourself.

And here's the major part of this: Once you understand that there are some things you're going to have to do on your own, make peace with that. Don't allow it to rip you up inside. Don't even build narratives around why you don't have anyone to walk alongside you in any particular season of your life. Just move forward. Because if you sit around waiting on somebody to save you, help you, partner with you, walk with you, or hold your hand, you just might miss the blessing that could have only come by the changes and chances that you took while leaping into your destiny.

One of the most life-changing parts of my story was one in which I had to go it alone—my decision to go vegan. I'd asked my family to do a thirty-day vegan challenge with me after watching the documentary *What the Health* on Netflix. After being sick for a year and seven months, with no answers from multiple tests and doctors, I decided to test the idea that a plant-based diet could possibly turn my health issues around. My family agreed to do the challenge, and we were off to the races.

After the first ten days, my chronic headache disappeared and I started feeling energized again. By week three, I felt better than I had in almost two years. On day twenty-nine,

I said to my husband, "I know we were only going to do the challenge for thirty days, but I think this is my life. I think I'm going to go vegan." My husband looked at me with so much love and sincerity and said, "Babe, I'm so happy to hear that. That's so good for you. But tomorrow? I'm going to need a piece of chicken."

So the next leg of my journey was mine alone to travel. And as scary as it was, I was willing to do it. Going vegan wasn't about my husband. It wasn't about my children. It was what I decided I needed to do to save my own life. I owed it to myself to be willing to put some works with my faith and go about my vegan business.

Honey, here's the thing. We come into the world separately. Even if you are one of twins, you still exit the womb by yourself. This means there are times when, yes, we do things in community, and there are other times when God calls us to walk our path with nothing but our trust in Him and a determination to finish. That first year of my vegan journey, I took the extra time to cook different meals to accommodate all the nutritional needs of my family. I researched various vegan cooking techniques and failed at more recipes than I care to admit.

Apparently, it was worth it, don't you think?

That walk alone is scary when you are a dreamer like me. I see and envision all kinds of things for my future and my family's future. While I love my husband and I'm so thankful for his love and support, he is one of those people who struggled for a long time with the idea of casting a vision for the future or dreaming big, seemingly impossible dreams. Somewhere along his own journey, he'd stopped be-lieving in the power of visualization.

So this is another area where I had to trust God and my-self alone. There would be many days when I'd say, "Listen, God has shown me this is going to happen. This is going to happen, Chance!" But he just couldn't get it. He'll tell you himself—he just didn't believe it.

While praying one day, I recalled a conversation with my mother that truly helped me when I was tempted to get frustrated because I had to dream alone. She'd said, "We can't get upset when we share an idea or dream with others and they don't get it. They don't get it because God didn't give it to them." Whew, that was instant relief for my soul, honey. God gave me the dream. It's not my husband's job to see it. It was my job to go after it. To live it. And, with or without my husband's support, to make it come true.

Needless to say, it wasn't long before my husband be-came a true believer in the way God was going to make my dreams come true. In a podcast interview my husband and I did for *The Love Hour* with KevOnStage and his wife, Melissa, Chance was asked, "What does it feel like to see all these dreams come to pass after not believing for so long? What does that mean to you now?" Chance's answer was simple: "I now know that God is real."

Listen!

What is better than hearing that? I could have been upset about Chance not understanding or believing in my dream. But that anger would have been sorely misplaced. It's not up to me to prove the power of dreaming. It's not up to me to do the transforming. It's only up to me to dream and then do. I know it's hard sometimes to believe that greater is coming. But when it comes? Ooh, God, we thank you!

There's another area of our lives where we may have to walk alone. And it's probably the hardest pill for any of us to swallow. In grief, we may find that we are left to grapple with the pain of loss in isolation. Not because we aren't loved or supported, but mostly because everyone grieves differently. What *we* need in order to process the loss of a loved one, friend, job, or pet may not be the same as what someone else needs. And not everyone will understand our process. It's unfortunate—because grieving alone feels so terrible—but still a heavy truth. We can't expect other people to understand how we feel unless they've been through it, and no one, not even siblings, experiences grief the same way.

So just like we have to release folks who don't want to go to the gym with us every week or don't want to go vegan with us, we also have to release those who don't understand what we're feeling when we're grieving. In short, it's not their burden to carry.

Yes, it's not just the lovely dream journeys we might take alone. Sometimes it's the hard ones and the sad ones, too. And collectively, they all refine us. They make us better humans.

That's it, honey. Everyone can't go. And I know that's hard to think about, let alone accept. When we achieve a success, we want to bring everybody with us. We get so excited that we think we can help every person in the world, right now, right away. I hate to say it, but that's the quickest way to tear something up—dreams, finances, and even relationships. We must remind ourselves that not everybody is equipped to come along on our journey.

And hear me: Yes, it's important to have support. Our communities are necessary. And yes, it's okay to bless people when we've been blessed. We absolutely should. But be discerning. Build a foundation that can't be broken. Build it solid and secure, and then—and only then—bring the right people along at the right time. But in the beginning? Don't be upset that you have to travel the road alone. Honey, some of the most successful moves you'll ever make will be ones you make by yourself. Be okay with that. I want you to win. You deserve it. We all do. You are worthy!

TSA

 Words are powerful. But we are the ones who give words their power. Stop letting words tear you to pieces. Ain't nobody even laid a hand on you and you're still letting those words— wherever they came from—rip you apart. Words do hurt. And it's okay to feel what you feel. But how you react to those words makes all the difference.

Some of you have allowed things people have said to prevent you from starting a business, or from going to see somebody you need to mend fences with. You've allowed words to stop you from being great. No one did anything to you. They just said something, and now your whole world has stopped. We're not doing that anymore, okay? You are more powerful than words thrown at you by people who mean to do you harm. [Talk to yourself. Say, *Those are just words, and I will not let them control me.*] We've got work to do, okay? Let's get to it. Start that business because you can. Call that person because you want to. Others' negative words don't matter. Go be great because you are. Go be amazing because you are. *You* give power to whatever you focus on. Those words aren't it, honey.

I CHANGED MY MIND
AND THAT'S OKAY

*"I am no longer accepting the things
I cannot change. I am changing the things
I cannot accept."*

—OFTEN ATTRIBUTED TO ANGELA DAVIS

Traditions are amazing, aren't they? Family traditions, work traditions, personal traditions; there are so many different types of traditions to be honored and treasured, if that's your business. However, some day you may decide to not participate in a particular tradition anymore. Maybe you have your own family and you want to create your own new traditions. Maybe you started a new job at a new company and they do things differently than your previous employer. Honey, that's okay. Just because it's always been one way doesn't mean it has to stay that way. "We've always done it" does not mean it has to continue to be done. You can start a new ritual or tradition, or you can say "I'm done with traditions" altogether. Either way, it's your business, and you don't have to explain yourself to anybody.

You've heard the saying, "'No' is a complete sentence"?

Let me tell you what's also a complete sentence.

I changed my mind.

And guess what? You don't have to offer any explanation. If you don't want to be part of a tradition, if it's not your thing anymore, then, honey, don't do it. The people around you—and yes, that means family, too—will have to adjust, and they will be just fine. You get to live your life by your own standards and define yourself for yourself.

And I realize that the family pushback is real. Hear this, honey. Just because "that's how you were raised" or "that's how Mom and Daddy did it" or "that's how it's always been" does not mean you have to keep on doing it. Okay? As a parent, I *know* we get it wrong sometimes. Whether we want to admit it or not, we parents don't always know why we do what we do. So just because you were taught a particular way doesn't mean that way is right for every season of life.

But how do I know if it is or isn't, Tab?

Check yourself. If you keep hearing from those in your circle of influence, "Why do you keep doing that? Why are you acting that way? Why did you even make that decision?" it might be time to reevaluate all those things you've "learned" and figure out if any of them are serving you well. Maybe they are, and that's your business. But maybe they aren't, and now you have an opportunity to shift your thinking and change the way you've traditionally thought or behaved.

Back home, going to church every Sunday was a real tradition for us. My parents became Christians when I was in the fifth grade. My dad had a drinking problem in my early years and was in a severe car accident. After literally dying and then being revived, he stopped drinking and gave his whole life to God. He was a changed man, which meant that our whole household changed, too. We all began going to church as a family. But prior to that, my parents would drop me off at my granny's house so that I could go to church with her down in Draper, North Carolina, just outside Eden. I would go with her and my great-granddaddy John, who lived right behind the church and was responsible for opening and locking the doors since it sat on his property.

Honey, it was right there at Great-Granddaddy's church where I learned how to play the tambourine. I'd sit on the front row next to him, a deacon, and tear my little hands up to the rhythm of the old gospel hymns coming through the Hammond organ.

This was our tradition. Church was mandatory. I went to Sunday school first, then the regular church service, followed by a second service. Don't forget Bible study on Wednesdays! And if you chose not to go to church, then best believe you'd be shamed for it. Even as a child, though, I never quite understood why, if God loved us so much, my granny or even my parents would make people feel guilty about not going. Growing up, the gospel's creed of "come as you are" became, in unspoken ways, "come when you're ready"—and that never sat right with me. We go to church because we want to "get right," but when we go, we're sometimes scorned because we aren't right already. Who's really ready? Neither perfection nor utter devastation should be the determining factors for seeking God and His solace within the community.

So guess what I've done with that tradition?

I've set it aside.

Yes, I honor how impactful that foundational experience was in my upbringing. But I do not believe that guilt and shame is the way to bring people closer to God. My immediate family does not go to church every Sunday. I vowed to myself from a very young age that if God blessed me to have children, I would never force a religion on them, or anyone else for that matter. I would present it to them. I would absolutely introduce them to God and ensure they knew that a relationship with the Creator is theirs to have. But in raising my children now, I don't believe I have to force them into belief or manipulate them into going to church with visions of hellfire and destruction. Because, honey, let me tell you something. The quickest way to turn somebody off is to try to force them to do something. That goes with church, yes, but it also goes with every other area of our lives. Relationships. Jobs. And as a vegan, I've seen it firsthand. Go ahead, try to tell somebody, "You need to go vegan or else!" and watch them roll their eyes and tell you to hush your mouth.

TSA

Stop talking yourself out of things, baby. Too many of us overthink everything. We write stories in our minds about why we can't do something and focus on it so much that we never actually move forward. I don't care if there's only *one* reason you might, probably, most likely be able to do something—focus on that one thing. Write the vision down. Make it plain. Set your goals, but be flexible enough to shift if the route to your destination changes. If one plan fails, create another.

Listen to me, honey. You are smart and capable. You are beautiful and talented. It doesn't matter how much or how little education you have; you know that life has taught you more than a few things. Use it all! Don't sell yourself short. Because here's the real catch: Whether you tell yourself you *can* do it or you tell yourself you *can't*, either way, you're right!

VEGAN PULLED PORK

I'm from the South, honey. Barbecue sandwiches with cole-slaw are a staple. So this is literally like a hometown favorite. I had to figure this one out. It just reminds me of home.

Oyster mushrooms, pulled apart but not cut (*the texture is perfect for this recipe, honey*)

Cilantro

A bit of chopped red onion

Orange bell pepper (*diced or strips, that's your business*)

Apple cider vinegar (*How much, Tab? Honey, what does your spirit say? Okay, do that.*)

Garlic powder

Just a dash of Liquid Smoke

Vegan maple bacon seasoning blend

Fresh lemon juice

Barbecue sauce (*I prefer Stubb's Smokey Brown Sugar BBQ Sauce, but use what you got, honey. That's your business.*)

For serving

Buns

Coleslaw

Avocado

Grab your pan and add the mushrooms, cilantro, red onion, bell pepper, vinegar, garlic powder, Liquid Smoke, and seasoning blend.

Sauté on medium for about 5 minutes or so.

Then add a squeeze of lemon juice.

See how it starts to brown?

That's when you add your barbecue sauce.

Scoop a bit out and add the mixture to your bun.

Throw some coleslaw and sliced avocado on the side, if you so choose.

Baby, you finna eat so good.

YOUR PERSONAL PRESCRIPTION

"Never be limited by other people's limited imaginations."

—DR. MAE JEMISON

The vision you have is yours, baby.
   Not mine.
Not theirs.
Not his.
Not hers.
Yours.
Let's talk about it. Are you listening?
Very good.
People who have to wear glasses will go to the doctor to

get a prescription, right? Some folks wear thick lenses, others wear the thin ones. Whatever the case, a prescription is particular to that person. If you try to give your glasses to somebody else to try on, what do you think their response is going to be?

"No, honey, I can't see through those."

Why? Because those glasses were prescribed especially for you. They can't see through them. They weren't supposed to see through them.

You see where I'm going?

God gave *you* that vision, that dream. Stop getting upset because other folks can't see it. God didn't give it to them. Just like those glasses, your dream is prescribed just for you and your vision. No one else's, alright?

Instead of spending so much time trying to force people to see your vision, invest your energy in manifesting that thing. Bring it forth. There is absolutely no need to get bent out of shape and argue about things other folks were never prescribed to see.

There's a saying that goes, "Every great dream begins with a dreamer. Always remember, you have within you the strength, the patience, and the passion to reach for the stars to change the world." I've been living my life this way for a very long time, and for a long time I would try to convince people to see what God had shown me many years before. It's only in the last couple of years that these people have been able to see what I saw. They believe now.

But that wasn't always the case. Take Chance, my husband. He is my number one supporter, right? He believes in me, and supports me wholeheartedly, okay? But as I've mentioned, if we're honest, when it came to me trying to explain my vision to him, he wasn't always that way. Honey, early on in our relationship, we had so many doggone arguments like that about me pursuing my dreams. I would tell him, "Listen, I've had this dream. God showed me something very specific. We're going to be big. I'm going to be famous. I'm going to be rich. I'm going to have all these things."

He couldn't see it.

I would meet people—folks I'd never seen a day in my life—and they would say things like, "Ooh, you have a calling on your life." Some were prophets. Others were just regular folks with discernment. I took those words as confirmation of what I'd known all along. And I would always try to tell my husband about this thing, this passion living inside me. I knew it meant something! But we would still argue about it. I'd still try to convince and persuade him: "You've got to believe. I'm telling you, I'm going to be this famous actor. I got this thing that is growing inside of me!" That's when Moma stepped in, remember? She told me that God didn't give my dream to Chance. God gave it to me.

So I took a different stance. I stopped trying to force my vision on other people. I held my dream close in my spirit and allowed God to continue to strengthen me. I grew closer to God and he strengthened my gift. I no longer felt the need to convince anyone of what I saw spiritually. I just let the dreams reveal themselves.

Everything God gives to us is not meant for other people to see. They may never see it or get it until you become successful and all the things come to pass, and that's okay! Keep working. Your job is to bring forth the vision; to manifest it. Just like my husband, the nonbelievers will eventually become believers, once it gets clear enough for them to see it. Chance says all the time, "Man, it's crazy. All these years, you would tell me these things were going to happen, and now we are literally living in it."

And that's the thing. Sometimes the people closest to you won't get it. It doesn't necessarily mean they don't love you. It doesn't mean that they won't support you, either. Sure, they might be calling you crazy along the way, but honey, that's quite alright. Be crazy! Some of us are big dreamers; we live in the sky. We see the possibility of the heavens. Others are more grounded. They deal with the tangible. The now. The practical. Guess what? We need both kinds of folks in this world. Chance and I are opposites, but it works because we create balance for each other. If I dream that I can touch the moon, honey, best believe I'm climbing on top of the house to try. Chance is there to say, "Babe, you're about to mess around and fall off this house, and then what?"

But here's what I want you to get: I'm asking you to stop trying to convince people that your dream or vision is real—but I still want you to keep speaking it out, loud and proud! Let people know what you have seen. Let them know what you are going to do. And let them call you crazy or unrealistic. That way, when you accomplish your vision, your dreaming is confirmed. They'll say, "Dang, she said she was going to do that!" or "Oh, wow. They said that was

their dream, and they did it! They are making it happen."
Yes, go on and speak those dreams out loud. You have to
share them with somebody so that somebody can validate
that you, in fact, had the vision. That it wasn't a fluke or an
accident but something you actually said you saw.

Baby, those are spirit glasses you're wearing. Don't waste
time being upset when somebody can't see through your
prescription! I promise you, it's okay. That vision is simply
for you. Go about your business making it manifest in the
physical world. And when you do, watch those nonbelievers
become dreamers, too. Watch them say, "You know what?
I'm going to try to do something, too." That's the blessing,
honey. That's the work.

6

EVERYDAY LIVING MIGHT BE YOUR LAUNCHING

"The most common way people give up their power is by thinking they don't have any."

—ALICE WALKER

W hat do you do for a living?"

We hear that question often, right? We might be at an event, and someone, trying to make small talk, will ask what we do. Or maybe that's a question we ask a new friend on a date. If I were to answer that, I could say, "I'm an actress," because I am. But there are other aspects of the question that are much more important.

In addition to being an actress, those in the social media world call me an influencer. All because I cook vegan food and share it with the world. But the most amazing part of that is, something as simple as me cooking right in my kitchen, for myself and my family, changed my life. I ain't nobody's chef, honey. I have never been in anybody's culinary school. And yet people hire me to cook my vegan food and tell my story. I've never been to school for communications or public speaking, and yet I lead panels, conferences, banquets, and festivals. I wasn't specially trained for any of it. And yet here I am.

What did I do? I lived. Living builds character. It shapes us into who we are going to become. I've been cooking now for over twenty years. Not professionally, just for myself and my family. I've made errors and tore up some meals, you hear me? But I kept on living. Kept on working to get it right. If I'm honest, I cook because I love to eat. And I love to feed my family. And guess what? God used that very thing to turn around and bless me.

Same thing with speaking. I loved talking to people. Being kind and sharing my stories of life with folks makes me feel good. So I started to share on my social media platforms. I wanted other people to feel like I felt. I wanted them to experience kindness and joy no matter what was going on at home when they turned off their computer. And once again, God used all of that to change my life.

Tab, what are you saying?

Honey, listen. If just simply being me and using the tools I acquired just by living could turn my life into the blessing it is, the same thing can happen to you. Kudos if you went to school and got a degree and are now working in your field. I'm proud of you. But that's not everyone's story. And I'm writing to *that* person right now. Baby, just because you can't afford to go to school or don't have the time to get that formal training does not mean your dreams will not come true. Look at your life. Sometimes the very thing you do on a regular basis with no thought at all—you do it like breathing—will be the tool God will use to transform your life.

Everyday living builds character. It sharpens that tool called life. It's everyday living that changed my entire world. For example, don't take being a mom for granted. You never know how learning how to cook for them kids, how to discipline them, how to change a diaper, and all the stuff that comes along with that will develop what you need in another area of your life. You don't know how God is going to use it. This degree that life gives you is everything, honey. And you can use it anywhere. Life will give you a master's, maybe even a doctorate, in whatever that thing is you're doing right now. Use that. Use your life experiences, okay? Let your life experiences make room for your dreams.

Simply living our lives every day is a gift. Stop complaining about it. *Why does God have me in this situation? What is it that I'm supposed to learn from this?* Honey, don't you worry about any of it. Your life might just blow your mind one day. I wake up every day saying, "Lord, is this really my life?" Because I have done nothing but be myself.

Now, don't get me wrong—I've done a whole lot of work. But that work came because I was being myself and doing the things I've always done. I've always cooked. But now I'm just cooking vegan food and people want to know more about it. I've always told stories. But I lived through those experiences and now people want to know more about what I learned.

Take the course called life, honey, and you'll find out how much meaning is in everything you've ever done. Every single thing you do has purpose, okay? I'm a witness to the fact that when you get a chance to look back at all that's happened, you'll see how everything you wondered about, were afraid of, or didn't understand was actually lining up like a perfect puzzle.

So when people ask me, "Girl, what did you do to be blessed like this?" I just tell them I was out here living. Working hard, being truthful, and sharing my story. That's really all I did. My soul woke up, realized that I was enough, and decided that everything I ever needed lived right inside me. So let me tell you this same truth: Everything you need is right there inside you. Let your life launch you into your destiny.

Part Two

HAVE THE
MOST
AMAZING
DAY

NO SHAME IN PUTTING YOURSELF FIRST

"Caring for myself is not self-indulgence.
It is self-preservation, and that is an act
of political warfare."

—AUDRE LORDE

The first rule of getting *to* happy, of reclaiming your joy, is to put yourself first. I know, I know. *That's easier said than done, Tab.* But how about this? Start today. Just one day. Don't worry about next week or next month. Today, do something to put yourself first. Decide to do what makes you happy. If you don't know what that is, take a pair of seconds to figure it out. This one day, I want you to do what makes you happy and see how that feels. Embrace that thing. Walk around in it. But here's the catch: Do not ever apologize for it. You should never apologize for trying to find your happiness.

I had to really learn to do all of that. And I continue to remind myself that it is a necessary part of living a free life.

There's always something that will intercept your decision. If you have a family, there will inevitably be some guilt lurking around your heart when you start taking back some of your time and energy. Don't buy into it! Of course, we have responsibilities in our home that we must attend to. If you have a partner or children, I'm certainly not suggesting you neglect them. But you also cannot neglect your own self. Filling your own cup means you'll have more than enough to pour out to those you love. But too often, we do that, right? And then we find ourselves frustrated and angry, lashing out at our family when it was really up to us to set boundaries and create moments for ourselves.

Two months into our first year in Los Angeles, I was working at Macy's while trying to pursue my acting career. I was hustling, going to auditions on my lunch breaks and scheduling photo shoots or small gigs whenever I could.

Sometimes on Saturdays I'd take an actor's workshop in order to gather more tools and study the craft. But the way it works here in LA, some of the best studying happens in the evenings during the week. There was one class in particular that I wanted to take, but it was on Monday nights from seven to ten p.m. I got off work at six, so this meant that on this one day, my husband and four-year-old daughter would not see me except early in the morning and late at night. I felt so bad about this. I kept thinking, *If I go to this class on Monday nights, I'm not going to be home to cook for my family. I'm not going to be there to put my daughter to bed.* And that's real, yes? I really didn't know how I could do both and make everybody happy.

That was my first mistake.

There are times when putting yourself first is not going to keep everybody happy all the time. I had to wake up one day and say, *Girl, wait a minute now! You done moved all the way to Los Angeles to pursue a dream. What you're not going to do is let this guilt stop you from studying the craft you moved here to pursue. It's a few hours on a Monday night. Your husband will be okay. Your daughter will be okay. They're not going to starve. If you need to, you can cook enough food on Sunday night that they have leftovers for Monday. Or here's a thought! Your husband can fix them something to eat. Go to that acting class.*

Yes, I had to have a whole conversation with myself. It takes that sometimes. Beat back those voices that are rooted in fear and insecurity—quickly!

And of course, everyone wasn't happy. Chance was angry at first. He said, "What do you mean, you're going to be gone from seven to ten on Mondays?" To be clear, it wasn't that he didn't support me. But he was used to me being able to do everything, always. He was used to me being home when I wasn't at work, cooking and cleaning, doing all the traditional things we'd both been taught, even after working a full day. He was spoiled. I did that. I remember my mama told me when I got married, "I'm going to tell you this—

don't start nothing you don't want to maintain, because they will always expect it." At the time, I thought, *You don't know what you're talking about, Moma.* Boy, did she ever!

At first, I felt like maybe I shouldn't take the class. If Chance didn't want me to go, then maybe it wasn't time yet. But deep down, I knew better. I had come to LA to pursue acting. Yes, I am talented, but just like anything else, the more you work on the craft, the more you sharpen those tools, the better and sharper you get. Not to mention the networking that is an absolute requirement in this town. Sure, I had spoiled my family before, but that didn't mean they couldn't learn a new way of doing things. Another thought took over: *Girl, no, ma'am. How he feels ain't your problem. You have to do this for you.*

So with all the love and respect in my heart, I said, "Hey, babe, I got to do this."

And I did. The first couple of classes were so exciting, but I was also a little nervous about coming home those days. Would everything fall apart while I was gone? Would my husband stay mad at me forever? No and no. Everybody got over it. It actually became our new normal.

That lesson is the one I share with you, honey. When you want to do something for you, go right on ahead. Do it because you deserve it. And don't feel guilty about it. Putting yourself first is not selfish. It's actually one of the most rewarding things you can ever do.

And guess what? Everybody will just have to deal with it. That's their business. Especially if they are people outside your immediate family. What those people think about you, their comments and "concerns" about the decisions you've made for yourself, ain't none of your business. Of course, be considerate. Be loving. Be respectful. But then handle your business and move on. Don't let guilt stop you. Don't let fear, that ugly "what if," stop you. Put yourself first. Do something great for yourself today. Then do it again tomorrow.

TSA

 Be open to encouraging somebody else today, because honey, I tell you this: When we encourage others, we are really encouraging ourselves. When we love on somebody else, we are loving ourselves. Be open to giving love as well as receiving it. *How do you do that, Tab?* Well, you have to start with filling yourself up with love and encouragement so you can give it out. Find a mirror and encourage yourself. When I used to work the night shift in a nursing home, it was nothing for me to go into the bathroom, stand in front of the mirror, and have a little conversation with myself. And when I came out, after filling myself up with love, I had so much of it to give to the people I was serving. It truly is a cyclical thing. Give people love, and they will give you love back, then you fill up on that love and give it back to them.

VEGAN CARNE ASADA JACKFRUIT TACOS

What do you know about Jack? Jackfruit, that is. Mexican food is one of my favorites. When I went vegan, I didn't want to miss out on it. Then I discovered jackfruit and have been rocking with Jack ever since. When I have that craving for Mexican food, jackfruit is my go-to.

A can of jackfruit in water or brine, drained and rinsed off really good
Carne asada seasoning
A little lemon pepper

Garlic powder
Fresh lemon juice
Tortillas *(hard or soft, that's your business)*
Your favorite taco toppings

Mango de gallo
1 mango
Fresh cilantro
Purple (red) onion
Red bell pepper

Fresh lemon and lime juice
Sea salt
Garlic powder
Diced jalapeño

Put the jackfruit in the pan and make sure the pieces are broken down real good.

Season the jackfruit with carne asada seasoning, lemon pepper, garlic powder, and lemon juice. *(Y'all gonna stop worrying me about these measurements, ya hear?)*

Sauté the jackfruit for about 10 minutes on medium. Cook it all the way down until it starts getting brown.

Scoop the jack into your tortillas.

Add your favorite toppings.

Oh, but wait . . . what's a taco without a good ol' pico de gallo?

How about mango de gallo? Let's make some.

Grab your mango, peel it, toss the pit, and chop it up.

Put it in your bowl, then add the cilantro, onion, and bell pepper to your bowl.

Add a little lemon juice and lime juice.

Add a sprinkle of sea salt and a dab of garlic powder, just a little bit.

And if you like a little spice in your life, drop some jalapeño in there—that's your business.

Stir and serve.

¡Oh Dios, te damos gracias!

8

PAY ATTENTION TO THE SIGNS

"When masks fall off, don't focus on where they fall, focus on who they reveal."

—STEVE MARABOLI

Baby, stop ignoring all those signs just because you don't want it to be true. We all have done it. We don't want to face the truth of something, so we pretend like it didn't happen or wasn't said. We ignore it because we hope that if we don't acknowledge it, whatever it is will go away. It won't. I know you don't feel like going through it, honey. Dealing with or facing it is going to be hard. But you will get through it. I promise.

When I worked in an office setting in corporate America,

I was used to being the only Black woman in the room. It wasn't just at one job; this was true with multiple employers. Before diversity and inclusion programs were a thing, this was the norm for many Black people in corporations all around the country.

At one particular company, I shared an office with two women who seemed really nice. In fact, I thought we'd gotten pretty close over the years we worked together. But at one point in my time there, little things started to happen that didn't feel right. Company emails would go out, and I wouldn't be included, but my two friends were. Or one of them would speak when I came into the room but the other one wouldn't. Or the office would fall quiet when I entered it even though they were clearly having a spirited conversation. I started feeling anxious about it, but then thought, *No, Tab, maybe you're overreacting.* I tried to make up excuses about why things were happening instead of facing what was right in front of me. The final red flag for me—the one that forced me to stop pretending that these women were my friends—was when I began to be obviously mistreated by the higher-ups, the supervisors, and my coworkers just ignored it or would gaslight me by saying I was making a big deal over nothing. I knew what being discriminated against felt like from previous experiences, but I didn't want to believe it was happening again. I had tried so hard to make everyone comfortable and to like me, but I was hurting myself in the process.

I eventually left that job, but in the back of mind, I still thought that maybe we were friends. My personality is one that always tries to see people for who they are and, in turn, to love and respect others wholeheartedly. We'd shared so much over the years. Surely we'd stay in touch, right?

No.

After I left, I never heard from them again. I tried to reach out. Tried to stay in touch. But they weren't interested.

That hurt. But it was a real wake-up call for me. I'd ignored the red flags—all those signs—that these women were never really my friends. Any sharing we did was out of courtesy. We just worked together, and there's a difference— one that will reveal itself when you leave that job. Not hearing from them afterward told me what I meant to them.

Friendships with coworkers are certainly possible. I worked at a call center from the late nineties through 2004, and there are people I worked with there who are still my friends today. But these women didn't want that. And that has to be okay.

My feelings were hurt, if I'm honest, because I allowed them to be. I chose to act like we were friends because maybe that's what I longed for. And sometimes when we operate out of our personal longings, it causes us to put on blinders. Our vision can become clouded by our desires to the extent that we don't see people or situations for who and what they are.

There are always signs. Pay attention to them. Some are small. Others are large and glaring. But honey, I know one thing for sure: If you choose to not see them because you are holding on to your expectations of what a person should be or what they should do or how a situation ought to pan out, you will disappoint yourself every single time. I expected those women to treat me differently. To see me differently. And those expectations didn't line up with reality. Honey, don't hurt yourself trying to pretend that something is more than it is. Remember, we can extend grace and love to people without hurting ourselves while doing so.

OKAY!!
you heard it
here, again

NOW IS THE TIME
TO FORGIVE

DEVOID : ENTIRELY LACKING OR FREE FROM

"He who is devoid of the power to forgive is devoid of the power to love."

—MARTIN LUTHER KING JR.

I f the global COVID-19 pandemic has taught us anything, it's that tomorrow is truly not promised. Let's stop waiting until we're sick, half dead, or barely making it before we make things right with the people we've had conflict with or significant relationships that have gone south. Make up with that friend now. Tell that person you forgive them now—or ask for forgiveness and mean it.

Forgive them, Tab?

I know, honey. Forgiving someone does not mean that

you must automatically be cool with the person. It doesn't mean that person got a get-away-free card. It does not even mean that you're giving them permission to be in your life. Forgiveness is strictly for you. It's for you to reclaim your power from that situation or that person. It is the ticket to your freedom. Some people get angry when they're told to forgive because they wrongly believe it means they have to go back. No, you don't. Forgiveness is for you. It has nothing to do with the person or the situation. I would never tell you to run out and put yourself in a position to be hurt again. It takes a lot of time, patience, and love to forgive, so definitely do it when the time is right. But please do it. The pain you are holding in your heart because of it is keeping you from your most amazing life.

To be clear: I'm nobody's pastor. I'm no preacher. I just live my life in obedience to the Spirit because that's what's proven to be true and worthy for me. I literally get sick when I hear something I'm supposed to share and don't release it. When I hear something or see something in my dreams or visions and I don't share it, my head spins. I get light-headed and nauseous. And I often have to lie down. But as soon as I say it, as soon as I get rid of it, I'm fine. I compare it to holding in something that was not meant for you. Like taking somebody else's medicine. If I take something that is not prescribed for me, it makes me sick because I'm trying to keep it.

For example, when I used to work at Macy's, there was this amazing little lady who worked on the receiving dock, where the merchandise arrives. This was during the time my mama was sick back in North Carolina and I would come and go, taking leaves of absences in order to help take care of her.

As the office manager, I was responsible for giving people their checks every Friday, and, of course, because I love to talk, I got to know everybody. Maybe not personally, but I said hello and knew their names. It was important to me to always be nice to people. And in return, I received that kindness back.

But one night I had a dream about Miss Stella. The only thing I really knew about her was that she worked at the receiving dock, and she was an older Black woman who reminded me of the women from back home at my church growing up. Just a nice, quiet lady. I've always been fond of those I consider my elders, and she was no exception.

In my dream, she had been opening boxes, and in an accident, had cut off two of her fingers. Her hand began to bleed profusely.

Now, by that point, I'd been studying dreams for some time. I wanted to know more about them because mine were so vivid. In college, I met a professor who shared with me how to study them and what some of the common interpretations might be. So I knew that when someone dreams of a person cutting a limb off, it generally means there's something inside the body that needs to get out. There's some type of sickness. Something is happening in there, and that person needs to seek medical attention immediately.

As I've said before, I used to be afraid to share these

messages. A person in their right mind would be skeptical if someone they barely knew said, "Hey, I had a dream about you. And in my dream, you cut your fingers off, and that means you need to go to the doctor." Most people are going to think, *Oh, Lord, that child is crazy.* That had always been a fear of mine when it came to telling people, especially strangers, about my dreams and what they mean.

When I woke up that morning, my spirit was disturbed for two reasons. One, I was concerned about Miss Stella, because I knew what the dream meant. But two, I was very afraid to tell her. So I decided I wasn't going to say anything. Nothing! *She don't know me, and I don't know her other than saying hello and giving her a check every Friday,* I thought.

All morning I sat in my office trying to work, and that thing kept bothering me. I started to get light-headed, but still fought it. *Nope, I'm not saying that. I don't know that lady.* And the moment I said it out loud to myself— "No!"—it literally felt like something pushed me out of my chair. And I knew at that point that it was an energy bigger than me and I had to get up and do what I needed to do. I got on the loudspeaker and asked for Miss Stella to call the office.

I didn't receive a call back immediately, so I went on the floor and started to look until I found her. I said, "Miss Stella, I know you don't know me no more than I know you, other than me speaking to you every day and giving you your check, but I have a gift I cannot control. I dream things, and sometimes I see or hear things. And I have messages I have to give." She just looked at me. She didn't seem to be disturbed by what I was saying at all. "You were in my dream last night," I continued. "I had a dream that you cut your fingers off, and that dream means you need to go to the doctor immediately. I can't tell you what's wrong. Just please go get a checkup."

Miss Stella turned to me and said, "Well, I haven't been feeling like myself. I've been very tired, and I thought that maybe I just needed to get more rest. But you know what? I'm going to go get checked out."

And that was that. One of the things about me releasing what I need to tell a person is that once it is done, I don't worry about it anymore. It's like I've done my job, and now I can have my peace back. I don't need credit for it. It's not for me. It's for the person. I'm just doing what God told me to do.

So I didn't think anything else about it. And about a week or so after delivering the message, I went on another leave of absence to stay with my mom in North Carolina for a couple of months. When I returned to LA and my job, I still hadn't thought much about Miss Stella. But then one day the office door opens, and in she walks. That's when I instantly realized, *Oh my God, I haven't seen her since then.*

She was completely bald.

Miss Stella walked in, dropped to her knees, and began to cry.

"You saved my life."

In the moment, I didn't know what to say. A part of me didn't understand what she meant.

"That day you told me to go get checked out," she said, "I did, and when they did all the blood work and everything, I was in stage three cancer."

I lost it. I never imagined it could be cancer.

She said, "I went into radiation and chemo instantly, and because of you, I'm still here."

I corrected her. "No, it's not because of me. It's because God chose me as a vessel." I was only the messenger. God loves us so much that he uses others to speak to us. I don't get any of the credit.

But I was very thankful for the confirmation. Because sometimes when you have a gift, you feel crazy. You also feel like other people think you're crazy when you begin to share. But that was confirmation for me that, again, I can't be silent. There were so many years when I would try to pray this thing away because I was scared of it. I lost friends because of it. And I couldn't control it. It comes and goes whenever it pleases. But I had to realize that that's how God intended it. He's in control of it. And only when it's needed will it come.

So, fast-forward to today, almost fifteen years later, I'm still using my gifts, and I'm not afraid anymore. And sometimes when I'm cooking live or when I wake up in the middle of the night to use the bathroom, God speaks to me and says, "Somebody needs to hear this." So I turn my phone on and I do a video and say, "I don't know who this is for." I'm not saying this because I just decided, "Oh, this sounds good." It's because God has given me something. I've heard something, and I need to share it.

Then I wake up, or after I'm live and I've said something that God has given to me to say, my inbox is flooded with emails from people all over the world saying, "Thank you! That message was for me." Or "I had been praying for God to give me some type of sign, some confirmation, and you gave it to me tonight."

Every time, I imagine it's God saying, "You ain't crazy, girl. You're doing my work. You're doing the work I have purposed you to do." I think the world—all of us—needs these messages. And together we confirm each other. They confirm me, and I confirm them. And at the end of the day, we all are just confirming what God has said to us, which is such a blessing.

So what are you saying, Tab?

Don't make yourself sick, baby. Stop holding on to that thing—whatever it is—that has you worn down all week long. I don't know if it's a person or a situation that has you tied up in knots. I *do* know that holding on to it will cause you to miss out on a whole lot of blessings. Confront it, so you can grab hold of all that's coming.

Some of us have been mad so long, we don't even know why we're mad anymore. We're walking around upset and don't know why. Let me ask you: What purpose does being mad serve? None, right? So feel what you feel, but don't get stuck there. Use your time to unpack the reasons why you're angry as opposed to just acting out of that anger. Then, when you step away from the mirror, get on your knees. Take that thing to the One who can do something about it. Praying is a powerful way to get the direction you need on the matter.

"Lord, release this thing from me. I don't know why I'm angry, Lord. I want to be free. Really, truly, free."

We are human. Which means we all will make mistakes. But because we are human, we're also able to love. We are able to forgive. We can help each other heal. We can't be healed if we don't tell anyone what we're feeling. If you don't have the conversation. If someone has hurt you or made you mad, you not only owe yourself respect, but you owe them the respect of telling them how you feel. Don't worry about what they might say or how they may respond. You did your part. You've said what you've said. The rest is the Spirit's work to do. Your healing begins with speaking your heart. Their healing will come when it's supposed to come. But nothing begins without those words. Whether they respond the way you want them to or not, it ain't about them. It's about you, living your truth and saying what you feel. In that moment, it's not about anyone getting your freedom, it's about you releasing that thing from your body and soul.

Go on ahead and pick up that phone. Get in your car and go to that house or office. Fix your thoughts and mouth to say, "Can I talk to you for a second? When you said [*insert offense here*], it made me feel . . ."

Unfortunately, we are living in a time when folks don't want to talk to each other face-to-face anymore. If they can't do it on the cell phone or post about it, they don't want to put it out there. We'll do that "vague-posting" where we'll post something hoping that one person will read it. Stop that. No more subliminal messages. No more lies about "Oh, that wasn't about you." Let's get back to looking a person in the face, and with the most love and respect, telling them what the problem is. Tell them how they might have hurt us. Maybe they don't know what they've done. Maybe they were going through something and off-loaded their pain to you without even thinking. We're not going to beat around the bush anymore, alright? We're going to be intentional with our movements, okay?

Very good.

It's exhausting to hold that stuff. It gets old, waking up mad every day. We're trying to be free here, and the best way to free yourself is to open your mouth. No, we're not lashing out at people. That won't work, and it will cause more problems. But we are sharing our hearts in a way that can be received. Because that's the work of healing and freedom.

I don't mean to make it sound simple. I know it's hard. We're conditioned to hold our peace. It's a generational thing sometimes. Moma didn't say anything. Daddy didn't, either. Grandma went to her grave with a few grudges and heartaches. Everybody around us might have kept stuff in. But those hurts and heartaches probably showed up in their bodies, too. Those grudges can absolutely turn into stress, which causes sickness, anxiety, depression, and cancer. What if telling the truth was the remedy to all that? Don't you want that cure?

So let's work on loving each other. Because, as I said, one day you might look up and somebody you love is gone. And you're going to be left here with that thing inside you, tearing you to pieces. That might be you right now. You didn't say what you needed to say when they were here, and now it is killing you. Release that. And while you can, be that person who says, "I don't want to do that to my family, my children, my mama, my daddy. I want all hearts and minds clear." We are creatures of love. God gave us a heart. A heart is designed to love—that is what it is for. So our natural ability is to love. And part of loving ourselves and those around us is being willing to forgive and be forgiven.

And maybe you start with yourself. Maybe the reason you can't say what you need to say to that person is that you haven't forgiven yourself. You haven't figured out how to love yourself. If you are not loving yourself, you sure enough can't love anybody else or truly accept love from others. It starts with you. Let God heal your heart. I know it's hard. No one protected you. That hurt you to the core, and now it has hardened your heart. But God can heal that. You just have to make the first step. Release it so that you can get your love back. So love can start making its way back to your family, your relationships, your finances, and your health. When you go talk to that person, be driven by love. Love heals. Love cures. God's love and grace are sufficient for us all.

Love that person who might be a little hard to love now. Give them the best of you. If the relationship means something to you, then the possibility of reconciliation is still there. And even if there is no possibility of reconciliation, you'll get to live with that weight off your chest. I told you, I want you to be free. And sometimes the very thing that's making you sick is that burden you're holding.

So let's stop waiting to get ourselves together. Let's stop waiting to make things right with those we love. In every aspect of life, let's eat right, live right, do right, and be right.

Let me be an example for you.

I love my stepfather dearly, but for a very long time, I was very angry with him. When my mama got sick, he got very angry with her. Some people do that, right? Not intentionally, I don't think. And it's not that they're really mad at the person who is sick. It's more about being mad at God because they feel wronged. They feel like God has given them a raw deal.

But unfortunately, my stepfather took his sorrow out on my mama. Prior to her getting ill, he was great. They had a very loving relationship. But he could not handle all that came with her sickness. Things were very tough, especially in her last year of life. She required a lot of attention and round-the-clock care. And he just seemed to not handle it well. He was there, but he wasn't. I remember interviewing Moma while she was sick because she'd told me that she wanted to tell her story. I offered to interview him also. In the interview, he was very clear about how angry he was. He was angry at her and at God.

I didn't know the degree of lashing out he was doing to my mother until after she passed away and I found the recordings she'd made telling her story. Moma said he would do things like put her in a wheelchair, because she could not move, and leave her there, even when he left the house. She wasn't close to a phone, so she couldn't call anybody for help, and if no one came over to help her get back into bed, she'd have to wait until whenever he came back. That was one of many things, large and small, that he did out of his frustration.

The amazing thing about my mama was that in her recordings, she still said, "It's not him." She said, "That's the enemy trying to get to me through him. But I know God has purposed me for this journey, and He trusts me with it. So I'm alright."

But I got so angry reading and listening to her talk about these different things he had done to her. It got to the point where I didn't ever want to see or talk to him again. I told him how I felt, and I was going to leave it up to God to deal with him.

But about a year and a half after my mama passed, I woke up one morning and forgiveness was just in my heart. I was literally brought to tears and overwhelmed with emotion. I realized I was not doing any good to him or myself by holding this grudge. I was holding myself back from prospering in life because I was holding hatred against him in my heart. I had been asking God for different things in my life, and they weren't happening. And that morning it was as if God was speaking to me and saying, "Listen, you can't live your life with hate inside you. You've got to live in a state of forgiveness. Even when the ultimate thing has been done to hurt you or your family, you still have to live in a state of forgiveness."

So I wrote my stepfather a long letter and told him I forgave him. And I truly meant it. I tried to call him, but his number had been changed. But I wrote the letter and mailed it off. That was in 2009. I didn't hear back from him for a good while. But a couple of years later, he showed up at my sister's house on Christmas Day.

My sister was on the phone with me when he knocked on the door. I could hear a deep baritone voice through the phone, and I instantly knew it was him. His voice was so distinct. Just hearing his voice made me so emotional, so when my sister put him on the phone, I cried my eyes out, because just the sound of his voice reminded me of my mama. It also made me so happy to know he was okay, that I was able to talk to him. That moment confirmed that I'd truly forgiven him, and I knew I was better because of it.

Months later, when we went home to North Carolina for a visit, I got to hug him and cry with him. I told him, "I have forgiven you. My mama had forgiven you. Now you have to forgive you." Because I knew he had been living with the guilt of what he'd done for so very long—maybe even still to this day—and that inability to forgive himself has caused him to get sick. But that is his healing journey to make. I simply remind him every chance I get just how much I love him. In fact, a few years ago, I posted a picture of us together, with the caption "This is what forgiveness looks like."

Yes, forgiveness is a real thing. First of all, you can't forgive anyone if you don't want to. It doesn't work that way. You have to live in a place of forgiveness. That's the only time you can truly forgive. Whether we need to forgive ourselves or others, we have to get about the business of forgiving so that thing doesn't live inside us and make us sick. No, it doesn't make the hurt go away all of a sudden. And it isn't a replacement for holding people accountable for their actions. But we all have to embrace the fact that sometimes we have to really forgive those who hurt us in order to be well ourselves. And you have to get to the place of really wanting to do that. Forgiveness is always for us. It's never for the other person. It's everything you need to keep moving forward with a sound mind and to have peace.

DO RIGHT
BY YOURSELF

*"Discomfort is always a necessary part of
the process of enlightenment."*

—PEARL CLEAGE

Sometimes the very thing that's necessary to have a *most amazing* day or life is the willingness to act quickly and decisively when something isn't right. This is especially true when it comes to our health. Honey, when are we going to stop waiting until we get sick before we decide we're going to take care of ourselves? We should not have to wait until we're sick before we decide, "I want to live!" We shouldn't have to wait until we've been diagnosed with diabetes, chronic heart disease, high blood pressure, all these different things, before we decide, "You know what? I want to eat right. I want to do better. I want to be better." Now is the time, baby! Let's take back control of our lives, y'all—yes?

To be clear: I was never someone you'd look at and say, "She's unhealthy." I was very mindful of how I ate. I worked out five days a week. But apart from that, I didn't treat myself well. For a long time, my focus wasn't on being healthy. I was interested in looking a particular way. When you do things solely because you want to look a certain way, you don't really care what you're doing to your body as long as you get that desired result. For me, I deprived myself as opposed to making better choices. Honey, I would take any diet pill or diet shot available if it meant I could fit into that dress I wanted to wear. I would starve myself for weeks or take laxatives and do all kinds of cleanses to try to flush out my system quick before an audition. I would terrorize my insides. And honestly, I think this behavior was part of the reason I got so sick. For twenty years, I did so much damage to my body. I deprived and overworked myself in order to feel good about how I looked, and at some point, my body must have said, *No, ma'am. No more.*

I've lived with off-and-on chronic neck pain since I was a teenager from a car accident I had in high school.

The story of how it all happened is actually somewhat funny, at least in hindsight. When I was sixteen, my aunt—we call her Sister because she's my daddy's sister—was working at Fieldcrest Mills in Draper, North Carolina.

She worked the third shift, from eleven p.m. to seven a.m., and she called me at seven one Saturday morning.

"I ain't got no ride, baby. Can you come get your auntie and take her home?" she said.

"Yeah, Sister. I'll come on and get you."

Mind you, I had on one of those long T-shirt gowns and not a lick of underclothes. Hey, I was very carefree, and I'm still that way to this day. I just threw on my little sneakers and jumped in the little brown Nissan pickup truck my dad had given me to drive back and forth to my new job.

It was only about a fifteen-minute drive to Draper to pick her up, and once I got down there, I took her to her home in Reedsville, which was about twenty minutes there and twenty minutes back. This is where things go left. On my way back, I said to myself, *You know what? I want me some wings for breakfast.* This was way before I was vegan, honey.

I was already on my street when I decided to go to KFC and get me some chicken. There was a back road nearby called Boat Landing where the boats would dock, and it was a shortcut that cars could take back to the main little highway. So I took Boat Landing to get my chicken and biscuits.

Well, honey, that road had the deepest curve in it, and when I took it, there was another car coming head-on. The car swerved to miss me but his back end caught my front, which caused my truck to flip up onto a hill. Had I flipped down, I would've tumbled into the sewers, and baby, I can't swim, so that would've been a tragedy. My truck ended up stuck on a fence, upside-down. Now, in my small town, everyone wore many hats. So my basketball coach was also a police officer. Coach Griffin showed up with the ambulance, and the paramedics had to use a sliding board to remove me from the truck and slide me down feetfirst onto the stretcher. But y'all remember that I didn't have any underclothes on, right?

Honey, I flashed every single one of them as they got me out of that car. Nevertheless, they finally stabilized my neck and spine with a brace and rushed me to the hospital. I'll never forget the look on my mama's face when she arrived in my hospital room.

"Didn't I tell you never to leave that house without putting no underclothes on?" she said.

Well, Moma, I didn't know. I thought I was just going to take Sister home. I just wanted some chicken.

So that began the story of my neck. The injury stopped me from playing basketball, and I was in physical therapy and visiting chiropractors for at least eight months or so afterward. For twenty-plus years after that, I would wake up with terrible neck and back pain. Later in life, I found out that I had discs dislodged in my spine and extreme deterioration because it was not treated properly in the beginning. I've been on a mission to self-correct ever since.

So I'd lived with the chronic pain of nerve and spinal damage for many years. The pain came and went. I'd wake up with a stiff neck that would last anywhere from a couple of days to a couple of weeks before it would right itself. So in 2016, when I woke up with pain in the back of my neck, I first thought, *Oh, I'm about to have one of my episodes.* But then it started to spasm. *This is different. Maybe it's just a muscle spasm or something.* But that same pain started shooting into the back of my head. It rested there, not for a day, a week, a month. That pain stayed in the back of my head for a year and seven months.

I never saw it coming. One day, things were going great. I had just come back from the Sundance Film Festival and things in my career were starting to move a little bit. I was doing stand-up comedy and having some fun. This time, there were no signs. Nothing in my life indicated that I was about to be laid out in a way I'd never been before. So when it did hit, I did what so many of us do. I went into a kind of denial. *It will go away in a few days.* It didn't occur to me to look at my past behavior, the way I treated myself and my body, as a possible source. I just thought, *This pain is worse than usual, but it'll get back to normal. It always does.*

Honey, it absolutely did not.

That pain pierced me every day. When it first hit, it took me completely out—from work and everything else—for two weeks. Then I thought I got it under control; I was able to manage the pain enough where I could drive and work again. But several months after returning to my nine-to-five, the chronic fatigue took over. Then I started having awful panic attacks on the job. I worked for four months in that pain before my body said, *No more.* I just couldn't do it.

When I got sick, Choyce was fourteen and our son, Queston, was three. Quest doesn't really remember too much about that time. He only knows about it because he hears me tell the stories. So I really thought I was doing a great job of hiding it. But my Choyce saw right through me.

I would get up in the morning and take her to school and Quest to day care. This was before I went out on full disability, so I was also still working. I'd sometimes have to take a week or two off, but then would muster up what little energy I could to get back. But I wasn't fooling my baby girl. She would say, "Mommy, are you okay?" And I'd say, "Yeah, girl. Mommy is just a little tired." But she knew something wasn't right.

For a long time, I'd even tried to hide it from Chance. And it wasn't until one time when I went to the bathroom in the middle of the night and had a severe episode that he knew something was really wrong. I got really hot and flustered and then, all of a sudden, very cold and drenching wet. Then my legs just collapsed under me. I could not walk. I fell to the floor and sat there for a while trying to figure out if I could pull myself up, so he wouldn't know. Eventually I had screamed for him to come pick me up and put me back in bed. Even then, though, I didn't want him to worry. Instead of asking for help, I did what so many mothers do. I was overly concerned about everyone else.

My husband has a very stressful job, I don't want to worry him.

The last thing they need to be concerned about is me being sick.

If I'm honest, a part of me was very worried about having ALS like my mom. Sometimes we believe because it happened to our parents, it's going to happen to us. And because some of my symptoms were similar, the thought sent my mind spiraling. Your mind is a powerful thing, honey. It can convince you that you have something you don't have. It will have you thinking death is around the corner or down the street. For me, I was afraid my husband would struggle the way my stepdad did and get angry at me for being sick. So I tried very hard to hide it, until that night when I couldn't anymore.

I thank God for that moment now. It was getting very tough to try to pretend to be okay at home. I was still pretending on social media, trying to post pictures that made it look like I was alright. I would even try to work out and hike—something that to this day is like therapy for me—on the days I could muster up the strength, then post pictures of that. My brother, Nick, would help me, even though sometimes I would fall down the hills because my legs would give out. We'd simply cry together out there and never tell anybody. He would help me get up there because he knew how bad I wanted to try to push through it.

But when I finally decided to come clean, my family was supportive. Maybe they, too, were glad to not have to pretend like they didn't know something was wrong. Maybe we were all relieved.

I went back and forth to the doctor, but there were never any answers. The doctors couldn't tell me anything.

That's when the depression set in. Because I felt helpless. I knew something was going on with my body. I was feeling sick. But when the doctors ran the blood tests, the MRIs, the CAT scans, everything came back normal.

"We're sorry, ma'am. We're sorry. We can't tell you what it is."

But this isn't normal. This isn't my normal feeling.

That depression took over, honey, and it got real heavy. But there I was, trying to act normal for my family and friends. I was caught off guard by this awful thing, and instead of dealing with myself, I kept trying to be what others needed me to be. It was exhausting.

I know that it wearied and stressed my husband, because at times he would just shut down a bit and get very quiet. That's how he handles things sometimes. And that, of course, would worry me, because I would be so worried about him not being able to focus at work. But still, we would come together and pray.

I also started to see Choyce grow up a little bit faster than I wanted her to, because she was so concerned about her mommy. On the days when I couldn't move my arms or legs, she would help me get dressed. She'd put my shirts on me when I was just too exhausted.

The good in all that was that I learned just how much I was loved. It was eye-opening to know that I had raised a child who wanted to help me and loved me unconditionally the same way that I loved my mama. I knew that with Chance, the very thought of anything happening to me was taking his breath away. It was causing him to almost lose his mind, because he did not want anything to happen to his wife. So despite it all, I'm grateful to know that I'm loved so deeply. We got through it.

Yes, I'm grateful for the vegan challenge setting me on

the path that turned everything around for me physically. But I'm even more grateful for the lessons I learned from that season of my life about taking care of myself in every way. Lessons I now have the privilege of sharing with you.

Sometimes in life circumstances will hit you and you will be woefully unprepared to deal with them. I didn't know that sickness was coming. But I also wasn't prepared for it. When I say, "Don't wait until you get sick to take care of yourself," that's exactly what I mean. Prepare yourself by being the best version of yourself today, baby. Instead of doing all kinds of terrible things to my body in order to look the way I thought I needed to, I could have just accepted me for me. I could have worked out for a stronger heart and healthy lungs and strong muscles, and not just to fit into a pair of jeans. I could have really taken time to make sure I was okay, physically and mentally, by putting myself first. Because I deserved that. And so do you.

But you know what, honey? It's not just about your health. That's my story, but it might not be yours. I've met people who say, "Oh, I would love to travel," but they never go anywhere. Even if they can afford it, they do what I talked about in a previous chapter—they talk themselves out of it. So in life, period, let's not wait until we *can't* do something to wish that we had. Whether it's eating better, taking a trip, or making up with a loved one, *now* is as good a time as any to make it happen. Life is too short. But life is also long enough if we live it right.

IT'S GOING TO HAPPEN

"There's always something to suggest that you'll never be who you wanted to be. Your choice is to take it or keep on moving."

—PHYLICIA RASHAD

Honey, here's what I know without a shadow of a doubt: Just because it hasn't happened yet does not mean it's not going to happen. Just because you haven't seen it doesn't mean it isn't coming.

What do you mean, Tab?

Glad you asked.

You're pregnant with something right now. Maybe it's the dream of a family. Maybe you want to start a nonprofit in your community. Maybe you always wanted to sing and make an album. Whatever it is, if you've begun to do your work, then it's in process. Just like a baby, in ideal circumstances—it takes nine months of incubation and nurturing to develop strong and healthy—your dream is going to take some time to develop. And even when the baby is born— say, when you finish that first song—they can't thrive on their own. You have to care for them. Raise them. Teach them how to be in the world. Well, that's also your task for growing your dream.

Nurture that dream. For me, that was and is studying my craft of acting. For you, it might be something else. Be brave enough to groom yourself and your dream to be what it needs to be in the world. Don't let your courage just live inside your keyboard. It's easy to post motivational and inspirational quotes. It might even be therapeutic to post all the good, bad, and ugly stuff going on in your life on Facebook. But none of that matters if you aren't doing something about it. If you do nothing but sit on the couch, eat chips, and look at what everyone's posting, then what was really the point of all that inspiration and motivation? Why did it not inspire and motivate you to get up and get to work on your dream?

But even as you nurture your dream and work toward its fulfillment, be patient. It may not look like anything is happening right now, but that doesn't mean the thing you are longing for is not on the way. Don't you dare allow discouragement to settle into your bones. Feel it, because it's definitely real. But then let it go as soon as you can. Choose to trust that God sees you and is working it out for you.

make the choice because its mine to make FAITH

Discouragement is like a disease. It can make you mentally sick. You'll find yourself so fixated on what didn't happen or what wasn't done that you eventually end up stuck in a well of negativity. And if you're not careful, that discouragement will show up in physical form—because our bodies are always listening—and it can take you right on out.

So many people look at my life and think, *Oh, wow. She's an overnight success.* Sometimes they even say it. What they don't know is that I've been pursuing my dream for twenty-three years. It would have been easy, and some would even say reasonable, for me to quit in year twelve or year eighteen. But year twenty-three was apparently my time, and I'm glad I kept on pressing.

I always knew I wanted to be an actor, and I acted in local and regional theater during my childhood and in high school; I also made clothes all throughout high school. So when it was time for me to go to college, my mom came to me and said, "Babe, I know you want to be an actress. I know that. But we don't know anybody who's ever done that before." She wasn't trying to discourage me. She was just teaching me what she'd been taught—always have a plan B. "Listen. You make clothes," she continued. "You're really good at that. How about you go to school to study fashion design? That way you have something to fall back on in case your acting doesn't work out. Or you'll also have something that can help you make money so you can pursue your acting." (This is probably why I don't believe in plan Bs now. Plan A will work for you if you truly believe in it.)

I did just what Moma said. I thought, *Well, I am good*

at making clothes. I do enjoy fashion. So I enrolled at the International Fine Arts College in Miami, Florida, to study fashion design.

In the first semester—I must have only been there for two months—I awakened in the middle of the night with one thought: *I'm supposed to be acting.* I knew I was wasting my time down there. And here's the thing: Nothing was going wrong with my classes. Everything was fine, actually. But I just had a call in my spirit; a passion that lived inside me that could not be quenched.

That night, at about one o'clock in the morning, I called my daddy. I know I scared him so much, calling that late, but I knew I needed to make that call immediately.

"Daddy, listen. I'm wasting your money down here. You need to come on and get me. I'm supposed to be acting."

And, of course, because I'm a daddy's girl, he did not hesitate. He said, "Well, it's Wednesday. I have to work at the mill Friday. But after I get off, I will get on the road." My daddy drove fourteen hours to Miami to pick me up.

Back in my hometown of Eden, I'm thinking, *Okay, Lord, what's next? How am I going to get to this dream I have?* After some research, I applied to the amazing performing arts program at Columbia College in Chicago. Mom and I flew there in the spring for a campus tour, and I fell in love with the city, the college, everything. It just felt right. "This is where I want to go, Mom," I told her. "I've got to go here and pursue my acting. This is it." I was so inspired.

So after being accepted, I prepared myself to start there in the fall. I decided that I would work my tail off all summer to ensure I had enough money to pay for an apartment and any books I would need come August. And that's what I did. I saved every dime I had and was ready to go start living my dream.

Then the bottom fell out.

Two weeks before the start of the semester, I received a letter from the school. Unfortunately, due to the financial aid I had received at the International Fine Arts College in Florida, Columbia would not approve my financial aid. And my parents were completely tapped out. I'd worked all summer long to save, and honey, I still didn't have enough for tuition.

It felt like someone had blown up a big, beautiful, colorful balloon, only to pop it right in my face. For half a moment, I let discouragement take over.

What now? What am I going to do? How am I going to pursue my acting?

Then I remembered my lifeline.

My mother was newly married, and my savior was my stepfather's sister. At least so I thought. Neither Moma nor I knew her very well. I certainly didn't know her other than talking to her on the phone a couple of times. But she lived in California. In one of those sporadic conversations, she'd said to me, "If you ever want to move to California, you can come and rent a room from me."

I asked Moma, "Do you think that's still an option?"

"Well, call her and see."

So I called her.

"Could I still come out there and rent a room?"

"Absolutely," she said.

Unfortunately, there was a lot she didn't say. She didn't say that once I got out there, she was going to make living there nearly impossible. She didn't tell me she was going to have me living in one room, with her two grown brothers and one grown nephew living in the den. All in a two-bedroom apartment where I shared the bills with her, but these men didn't contribute at all to the household despite taking up space. She didn't tell my nineteen-year-old self any of that.

Nevertheless, I'd made it to California. Sure, it wasn't LA; I was living in the bottom of Orange County. Beautiful, but nowhere near Hollywood. Nowhere near the places where my dreams could come true—but closer than I was before. That had to count for something, right?

Honey, it was beyond hard. I had to work two jobs to afford to even live there. I'd just started seeing Chance back in North Carolina, and he was planning to come out to California with me so we could get our own place. I couldn't tell him about the bad living situation. I held my dream tightly, so I wasn't going to tell anybody anything. I was just going to figure it out.

After I'd been there for a couple of months, Chance arrived, and he was immediately upset. "Wait a minute! This is insane, Tab! This lady's taking your money, and you got other people living here. All you really have is a room, but you're paying all these bills?"

Then he said the thing I didn't want to hear.

"The cost of living is way too high out here. We need to

move back to Greensboro, to North Carolina, stay for one year, save up our money, and then move to Los Angeles so you can really pursue your acting career."

He was right. And I agreed to move back home. But I couldn't help but feel that familiar weight of discouragement in my heart.

Oh, God, I'm leaving California. I have to wait another whole year before I can really start trying to do what I love. This hurts.

Well, honey, let me tell you about that one year. That one year turned into five. In that time, me and Chance got married, and we had our daughter, Choyce. We both had good jobs, and we had a house.

And deep down in my heart, where I'd pushed it aside, there was my nearly forgotten dream.

I have a child now. Responsibilities. I certainly can't pursue an acting career now.

When you're from a small town like Eden, there is a certain mentality—expectations that people live by. You get married. Go to work. Have babies. Y'all get yourselves a house and live happily ever after. And there's nothing inherently wrong with that. Some people dream of that life, and I'm not mad at them. But the limitations of that mentality also mean that ain't no big dreaming happening. Which means that those of us who want to do more, go somewhere else, and do other things can easily get stuck. And as much as I didn't want to be stuck, I started to buy into the idea that my life in Greensboro was all there was for me. I really stopped dreaming. I stopped thinking about acting. I was working at a UPS call center as a supervisor. Our life was pretty good. So I tucked my dream deep down and figured that my life had chosen my path for me.

We had a cute little redbrick house in Greensboro, a stone's throw from Eden. There was a huge baseball field next to us and a small church across the street. We were surrounded by family, and so much love and support. Everything was going well, and I thought I was okay with it all. But then one morning, I experienced what can only be described as an earthquake. It felt like my room shook wildly and I woke up startled. Then a voice like thunder was so loud.

"This is not the life I planned for you."

Oh my God. Lord, is this you speaking to me? Because if it ain't, I'm about to send myself to the crazy house. I'm about to lose my mind.

I got on my knees and prayed, *Lord, if this is you speaking to me, please, I need a sign today. I need you to show me clearly that this is you.*

I wanted the confirmation so bad, because as soon as I heard "This is not the life I planned for you," it instantly brought back in my spirit, *You're an actor. You're an actor.*

But I was in Greensboro, North Carolina, so becoming an actor still felt so far-fetched.

How, Lord?

Later that day, Chance, Choyce, and I were on our way to the mall. As we were driving, DJ Busta Brown came on the radio and said, "Hey, y'all. This is Busta Brown. I've got a new TV show on the WB network. And I'm holding auditions for a female cohost."

Honey.

Honey!

I almost tore the windows out of the car. I was going crazy because all I kept thinking was, *That's my sign, right? That's my job!*

It's hard to tell people about hearing the voice of God. If they've never experienced it or they're not a believer, they will look at you like you're crazy. Even if they're your partner or a family member, it will sound strange to them. But I didn't care! I was clear that I'd heard what I heard. And in that moment, I had my confirmation.

The auditions were at a Jamaican restaurant in Greensboro. It was a weekly audition show, and each week, people were eliminated until there was a winner.

During the first audition week, there were probably thirty or forty women there waiting for their shot. We had to introduce ourselves in front of a crowd and say why we wanted the gig. After that first week, I got the callback for the next week's audition where we had to pitch a segment that we'd produce for the show. It was now down to ten women. I pitched the idea of a fashion show with local designers. I loved fashion, and I had a girlfriend, Tina Bennett, who would redesign clothes. I called her and said, "Hey, I'm doing these auditions for the Busta Brown show and I have to produce my own segment. I want to show local fashion designers, and I want you to do a little fashion show during the audition." She was on board!

Honey, we got a couple of models and took some vintage pieces of clothing, cut or painted them, and re-created looks with them. We did the show in the back room of our house in Greensboro with me hosting and a camera guy, Carlos, shooting it for me. I showed the segment at the next Busta Brown live show, and that solidified me making it to the final round with two others.

The very last week of auditions was the "give back" episode. We were tasked with going to a place that was giving back to the community and interviewing the organizers. Well, honey, that was right up my alley. I passed that test with flying colors and ultimately ended up winning the competition.

Whether I was hosting a live party or going behind the scenes at a concert, I had so much fun working on the show. It just gave me confidence, and it fueled the fire inside me. This was another affirmation of my gift. Working on the show gave me the desire to say, "Okay, I'm ready to go back to LA now."

That gig did one thing for me—it taught me how to start dreaming again. I interviewed everyone from LL Cool J to Nas to Junior M.A.F.I.A. and Lil Jon. In addition to interviews, I started producing television and my own little segments like the fashion show I'd presented at the audition. I started doing community theater and short films. I drove three hours to Wilmington, North Carolina, to do extra work on the hit TV show *One Tree Hill*. All of this awakened me to the possibilities. It was time.

"It's time for us to move back to LA," I said to Chance. "I know it's been years, but I have to go."

He said, "No, we're not moving back."

I knew his reservations. I understood his fears. But it wasn't an option for me.

"Listen, I've heard the voice of God, man."

He wasn't moved.

Then I said, "Okay, I'll tell you what. I'll go on my own. I'll fly back and forth. Something is calling me. God is telling me, 'It's time to go.'"

Of course, he wasn't interested in the back and forth.

"You ain't going to be going back and forth without me. Let's figure this thing out."

And we did. We spent the year planning, and on Halloween 2004, five years after our first attempt, we moved to Los Angeles. I could feel the passion pulsing inside my heart.

Now I'm in LA. This is where I can get started.

As I've shared, I took a job at Macy's and began auditioning. I was on my way, right?

Well, no sooner had we gotten settled than my mom started to get sick back in North Carolina. She was then diagnosed with ALS, also known as Lou Gehrig's disease, a terminal neuromuscular illness. My world stopped. My dreaming stopped. The dreams of becoming an actress stopped. You only get one mama.

I flew back and forth to North Carolina to help care for her for weeks and sometimes months at a time. Early in her illness, she'd get mad at me flying in from Los Angeles to take care of her. She'd say, "Why are you here? You're supposed to be doing your acting out there in LA." And I'd say, "Moma, no. That time will come, but right now, it's my last little bit of time to spend with you. This is where I want to be." I would also remind her that if the tables were turned, she would be right there by my side.

It was so hard to see my mom literally lose herself to this disease, but I had to be there. Nothing was more important than helping to care for her with my sister. And I didn't know it at the time, but God was using the experience to teach me some things; to equip me with what I would need to be not only a better actress but a better human. I learned what it meant to have patience. To have empathy and to show love. I was forced to be more vulnerable than ever before in my life.

When my mother passed away in 2007, I was more determined than ever to do what I was called to do. There was no way I could watch my mother fight to live and lose her battle, experience that life-changing grief, and not pursue my dream with every piece of my heart and soul.

The loss gave me new motivation. It gave me a fight inside myself, and when I returned to LA, I jumped right into it. I would say yes to almost anything. I did five straight-to-DVD movies, commercials, and music videos, even if it was for free. Moma wanted me to make it, and I was going to do just that. While I didn't have any big breaks during that time, I was so grateful for the small victories.

Chance and I bought a home in Palmdale, which wasn't the best move. We were suckered into living in the desert because my husband is a police officer and the other police officers and firemen he worked with all said, "Man, we all live out there." They sold us on it being safer to live out there, and we believed them, despite the fact that we'd lived in LA for five years and never had a problem. (We've now lived in the Valley for ten years and never had a problem.)

While we were living in Palmdale, I worked as a caregiver in an assisted living home. The auditions began to dry up, and my old buddy discouragement paid me a visit.

God, I feel like I'm getting further away from acting. Things were going so good, and now everything has disappeared. Lord, what's going on?

Palmdale wasn't the best experience for us, and so after a year, we headed back to LA, to the Valley. Chance and I were also talking about having another baby. Ironically, though, I didn't have the same concerns about the impact of having a child on my career as I did years before. Having Queston was a decision. Choyce was a surprise.

Before I got pregnant with Choyce, I was on a birth control pill that was giving me headaches. So the doctor changed the dosage and brand for me, but said I needed to clear my system out for thirty days. Well, honey, after those thirty days, when I went back to get the new set of pills, I was pregnant with Choyce.

We were so young then. It was certainly not planned. Chance already had a daughter, Ty-Leah, so I was concerned. *Oh, God, two kids before you're twenty-two.* It was very stressful. Remember, I was still hoping to get back to California, and now all of a sudden, I'm pregnant. I thought I would have to forget about acting; that because of my new responsibility, the dream was too far away to reach. With Queston, it was a bit different.

When my mom was sick, I'd go stay with her sometimes.

She was on a ventilator for the last year of her life, and during the night I would check her numbers and make sure she didn't need to be suctioned. There was one time when I woke up to check on her as I always did, and this one particular night, she was glowing and smiling so hard. She had happy tears streaming down her face.

I said, "Moma, what in the world are you doing awake? It's like three o'clock in the morning."

She said, "You know what? God just showed me what he's going to do in your life, and it is absolutely amazing."

"Really? What is it? Can you tell me?"

She said, "I can't tell you. But I will say that before any of it happens, you will have a son. He's going to have my eyes." Then she just laughed and laughed.

And you know my mama was never wrong, right?

I had no desire to have any more children at that moment. We had the two girls and that was enough. We didn't think we could afford to have any more kids. Chance and I both just wanted to pursue our dreams in LA. But about five years later, we both woke up on the same day, looked at each other in the bed, and said, "You ever thought about having another baby?" We literally had the exact same thought at the exact same time.

"I would like to have another baby," I said.

"I would like to try for a son," he said.

I wasn't even thinking about what my mama told me. It just felt like the right decision to make. Together, we said, "Let's do it!" See, at that point, I'd lived a life that revealed that God was always in control. I'd loved and lost

and loved again. I'd seen highs and lows and highs again.
I believed that nothing could stop my destiny. So I told my
husband, "Listen. We're going to have this baby, and after
a year, after the baby turns one, if it's meant for me to be
an actor, God will show me."

I said "after the baby turns one" because, honey, when
I'm pregnant and first have my baby, I like to be home for
that first year with the child. I don't want to be out and
about. I like to be present at every turn.

My son turned one on March 18, 2013, and on March 19,
I got an offer to do a movie with comedian Tiffany Haddish
before her amazing *Girls Trip* break.

By the time I had Queston, I'd lived a little bit. I was
wiser and had learned to trust God for everything. As a result, I was less concerned about the impact having another
child would have on my life. Plus, my mama told me these
great things would happen in my life, but not before I had a
son. I understood that it was a gift to even be able to have a
child. And to do it twice—my goodness, I was just grateful.

I was so excited to be on that feature set doing the thing I
loved so much. But after shooting wrapped, things got quiet
again. I was auditioning but nobody was calling back. I was
also working a nine-to-five, because the plan to return to
acting full-time was halted. Once again, I felt stuck.

Hey, discouragement. You wasted no time this go-around, huh.

I was working my nine-to-five, doing hair in my home on
the side, taking classes at night, working on my stand-up on
the weekends, and still squeezing in auditions and whatever
else I could. I was exhausted and burning out.

Is it going to be like this forever? Am I going to get stuck in this job and never be able to act like I want to because I have all these new responsibilities that need money?

Let me tell y'all something. God has a way of doing things. Of course, I never, ever wanted to get sick. No one ever wants to get sick. Not being able to work because of my pain meant going on disability. But it also meant I couldn't really audition. As I've said, the unexplained pain in my body made me depressed. Honey, that pain in my heart sent me spiraling.

God, you've got to take me out of here. I don't know what's going to happen, because I'm not well.

The rest is internet history, I suppose. After going vegan and mentally and physically healing, I was driving for Uber, and one day I posted a video that went viral and changed my entire life. None of that was planned. But what was I doing? I was working while I was waiting. I was driving for Uber while I was waiting for God to show me the next step.

Why do I share all this with you? Because I want you to know that trials will come. And, honey, discouragement will surely try to move into your mind and heart rent-free. Don't let it stay too long. Even if something hasn't happened for you yet or you keep getting knocked off course in pursuit of your dream, God is going to use everything for your good. All those years of ups and downs built character inside me. Caring for my mom, for other people, working third shift, making ten dollars an hour, the year and a half of sickness—every single thing on the way to these chapters of my life built my character. Most important, they

Romans
8:28

helped me to become who I needed to be today. I'm able to understand people who are going through sickness or who have anxiety and depression. I lived through it. I understand what it is to be discouraged. To feel like it ain't ever going to happen. But I'm here to tell you that every single thing I went through built me for this moment.

It's okay to be discouraged. It's natural. But in the discouragement, find your courage. Find the courage to keep going. Very good things don't happen overnight. I'm a witness, honey. Remember, it took me twenty-three years. A friend of mine once said, "Can you imagine if, twenty-three years ago, God said to you, 'Listen, I will give you every dream your heart desires, but I need you to give me twenty-three years.' Would you have said yes, or would you have said, 'That is crazy! I ain't going to wait no twenty-three years'?"

There's no way for me to know the answer to that. But I do know I did it. Even when I tried to give up, the call on my life was so strong. That thing that lived inside me would continue to jump out and grab me again and say, "No, you've got to keep going!"

Honey, it's okay to have a long time to wait before your dreams happen. But while you're waiting, keep working. Keep believing. Keep praying. Never stop dreaming. Allow the times when you're discouraged to fuel you so they push you forward. There's nothing worse than being discouraged, in pain, and sad, and not doing anything about it. It's too easy to sit in that forever and ever. It's such a disservice to you and your gift. Keep working. Take care of yourself,

[handwritten note: what to do while waiting]

and never stop believing. That's the part that will prepare you for when things start to turn around. If you work while you wait, when it is your time, you will be ready.

heartfelt this in your spirit today, didn't, we okay! TSA

 When you have started a business and you are a one-person show doing everything yourself, it can be very frustrating. Some days are just so discouraging. Ask me how I know.

In doing what I do, I've had both life and work interruptions—like moving and production schedule changes—prevent me from doing things with the kind of consistency that I like. I've had my car broken into and products people had sent to be featured on Very Good Mondays (a social media video series I produce with my daughter, Choyce) stolen from it. I even went to launch a new T-shirt line and during the test run, realized that all my work on the design had disappeared from my computer. I've broken down crying over some of my challenges in business. I've cried out in prayer, "Lord, what else do you want me to do? Why do things have to be so hard?" So I know how tough it can be to grow something from scratch and deal with all the trouble that comes with that.

But I want you to take a minute, breathe, and remember that old saying: To whom much is given, much is required. There will absolutely be moments when things don't go right. You will have your fair share of breakdowns. It's 100 percent okay.

Just don't live there.

When things aren't going right—maybe you're running late or something you're trying isn't working out—remember, honey, you're not curing cancer. (Unless you are, then go on about your business.) But you're probably not doing anything that should keep you in a panic.

Just breathe. Then breathe again. Then breathe a few more times. Say a little prayer and release all that frustrated energy. Then think about what the lesson is. What do you need to take from this? Are you wearing too many hats and need a bigger team? Okay, put that on your list. You might not be able to put that in place now, but this experience just showed you the plan for the future, when you go to the next level.

So if you are a small business owner and it feels like things are falling apart, stay in there. The payoff is coming.

12

GAB #1

RUNNING ONLY LEADS YOU BACK TO YOU

GAB #2

"It's time for you to move, realizing that the thing you are seeking is also seeking you."

—IYANLA VANZANT

GAB #3 → now um ~~uncertain~~ but so excited because um ready

Baby, it's time to stop running. You know what I mean. Aren't you tired? You want the most amazing life but don't want to face the things that prevent you from having it. You can't keep running from your problems, because eventually they are going to catch up with you. It really is a waste of energy. Face that thing. It's the only way you're going to get through it.

When my mother was sick, I had a big falling out with my older sister, Tasha, who I love dearly and who is amazing.

In the beginning, when my mama first got diagnosed with ALS, she was only given six to eight months to live (she went on to live for three years). I was in California, and my sister lived in our hometown, only eight to ten minutes from our mama. But she wouldn't go and check on her as much as I thought was needed. It felt to me like she'd just decided, "I'm not going to go see her. I don't want to deal with it." In hindsight, I know she was dealing with her own grief, in her own way, but we had it out. I was so angry with her, because I was out in California and couldn't be there every single day. Sure, I would come and go for weeks or months at a time, but she was *there*. I was depending on my sister to step up.

But you see, the problem was, I had these expectations without ever thinking about how she might be handling the pending loss. Without considering that people process things differently. I'll never forget having a conversation with my mom, because I was so angry with my sister, and Moma saying, "Listen, you don't handle things the way your sister handles things, and your sister doesn't handle things the way you handle things." My sister's tendency is to run, because to her, out of sight is out of mind. If she runs from it, maybe it doesn't exist. That's what helped her manage such overwhelming despair; she didn't want to accept our mom's illness. Neither did I, but I suppose I was more of a realist about it. However, like Moma said, that was *me*.

"When the time comes," Moma said, "she will accept it and come around."

If I'm honest, I didn't want to wait for her to accept it. *Moma needs help now!* My stepfather, unfortunately, had all but checked out; he didn't want to deal with it, either. It was a very tough time. But after talking to my mother, I just tried to release my expectations.

And, honey, guess what? My sister sure did come around. In fact, she turned out to be the best caregiver ever to our mother. When I wasn't there, I never had to worry, because I knew my sister had it.

That experience taught me a couple of things. First, we can't expect people to handle things exactly the same as we would. People run because of fear. They run because of frustration. They run out of a deep sadness, anger, confusion. Most of the time, it's not because they don't care. It's likely that they're trying to figure out how to deal with it. We get so upset with a person who runs—even when that person is us—that we never stop and say, "Wait, why are they running? Why am I running?"

And that's the second lesson: The way to stop running from our challenges is to be willing to unpack why we are running in the first place. Dig deep. Ask, "Why do I do that? What did I go through in my past that caused me to feel comfort in running?" That work might be long and hard, and might be helped by talking to a professional counselor, but it's worth it in the long run.

Some of you might be running from your dreams. You were born with this dream inside you, but life done got in the way. Honey, know this: You can't run from it. Your dream will lace up its sneakers tight and chase you down *just prayed this away a couple pages ago*

G.19.

until you face it. It won't feel good. In fact, it will probably be uncomfortable. But sometimes you have to be made to feel uncomfortable before you'll turn around and say, "Okay, I'll do it. Stop chasing me. God will make your life uncomfortable until you face the thing that has been tapping at you, the thing you've been running from. Once you do, you'll begin a whole new journey of releasing the fear. Minute by minute, day by day, week by week, month by month, and, yes, sometimes year by year. But if you're committed to it, you'll soon realize it wasn't even the problem that you were running from. You were running from yourself. You were running from your own insecurities, the what-ifs and fears; your own doubt. And the moment you face it, your entire world begins to change.

"YOUR MIND"

Will you stop running overnight? Absolutely not. Like I said, it's work. Sometimes we don't even know where to start because we have never seen it as running. Removing layers that could have taken years and years to accumulate takes time. But oh, honey, there's freedom on the other side of it. You'll start to feel more strength than you realized you even had. You'll start to be open to things coming your way. You'll be less fearful.

• *compliment*
• *attacked*
• *greatest weapon*

The work will change you. I know it. I saw my sister transform into this powerful woman, and it was such a beautiful thing to watch. And I went from being so frustrated and angry to more understanding. I learned that everyone comes to it in their own time.

Don't be quick to judge them or yourself, baby. Give them and yourself permission and time to grow.

VEGAN SKIRT STEAK

I haven't had a steak or red meat in over twenty-five years, so I came up with this recipe because many of those who follow me on social media requested. Also, my sister loves steak, but I know that steak doesn't love us—not my family's blood type. So I figured if I can make this and she liked it, maybe she'll stop eating steak. Honey, she's still eating it, but that's her business.

Portobello mushrooms *(a little or a lot, because that's your business)*
Coconut aminos
Garlic powder
A little onion powder
A splash of white vinegar
A little black pepper
Melted vegan butter
(Now, I told you not to ask me how much. Cook by the spirit, baby.)

Slice the mushrooms up into thin rounds and put them in a bowl. Mix up your spices and then add your slices. *(See! Tab got bars!)* Mix in the butter. Dip the mushrooms in for a little bit, or you can let them marinate, whichever is just fine.

Place your mushroom slices in a cast-iron skillet—let that marinade drip off just a little first—and sear on medium heat.

After a few minutes, flip them over.

Oh, God, do you see that?

Warm up the marinade and pour whatever you got left on those mushrooms.

Add your favorite sides, like green beans or some mashed potatoes.

Lord, have mercy.

Part Three

DON'T YOU DARE GO MESSING UP NOBODY ELSE'S

When God
is in it and for it
he prepares the way
with all the tools!

Be Encouraged
you have everything
you need.

Him

SHOW UP
AND LET
THE BLESSING
BE THE
MOTIVATION

*"You don't make progress by standing on
the sidelines, whimpering and complaining.
You make progress by implementing ideas."*

—SHIRLEY CHISHOLM

Whenever I'm having one of those moments when I
don't want to do something, I remind myself that

there was a time when I *couldn't* do it. There's something about sitting in gratitude that pushes you when you need it. I encourage you to let your blessings be your motivation to do the things that you don't necessarily want to do. Because, honey, the blessing is the fact that you still *get* to do it.

My mom used to say, "I don't look like what I've been through," and that's 100 percent true for me. I'd bet that if you took a moment and looked back over your life, you'd realize that it's true for you, too. But we have to be careful with that, also. Because we know how to show up and look good. We know how to play the part and present ourselves in a way that hides the journey. And, of course, people buy into the look. They believe what they see. And it's easy to convince them that we're alright, that we're good, when we're not. That's when the saying becomes less of an affirmation of our healing and more of a way to hide our pain.

That's why I firmly believe it is our job as humans to take the time to check in on each other. I don't care how good someone looks; they could be falling apart inside. I don't care how well they are dressed or what car they drive; they could be one paycheck away from being homeless. Baby, it does not matter what someone looks like on the outside, if you never take the opportunity to get to know the person on the inside. So let us all be mindful that just because someone looks amazing doesn't mean they haven't been through something. A diamond may come from coal, but it's cut to shine and be beautiful. Yeah, we are all diamonds, but what in the world do we have to break through to get to shining?

Very good?

Very good.

The neck pain—stenosis—that I still deal with as the result of my accident did a tremendous amount of damage to my spine. The top of my spinal cord is deteriorating, and that comes with a great amount of pain. I manage it very well now because I have been introduced to healthier options—food, supplements, and therapeutic modalities—for dealing with the inflammation and pain, but it is not gone completely. Some days I still wake up in a lot of pain—but what do I do? I put my face on, fluff Donna up real good, put on a cute dress, and go to work.

But here's the thing: Just because you see me in my dress and earrings smiling doesn't mean I'm not hurting. Doesn't mean I didn't want to sleep in. It means that despite everything, I showed up. I remembered a time when I couldn't get out of bed and decided that because I could, I would.

Now, be clear. Tab isn't saying to ignore your pain. I'm not saying for you to forgo rest and relaxation when you need it. Lord knows we all need to have more balance in that regard. But I *am* saying that once you can manage whatever it is that's causing you trouble, figure out a way to show up for yourself. Don't let it take you out of here, you hear? Sit in gratitude that the pain is not as bad as it could be, or as it once was, and use that as your motivation to propel you forward.

And don't forget that nearly everyone around you is doing the same thing.

Everyday people are showing up for their lives. They do it because they have partners and children counting on them. They have jobs to be done. That's life, right? But let your own "showing up" build empathy in you, so that you can turn around and check in on the next person. It only takes a minute to stop and have a little conversation. "How are you? You alright?" goes a long way when folks are smiling through their pain.

Let us be better humans when it comes to this, yes? Check in with yourself, and once you know you're good, go on ahead and check on somebody else.

Honey, you want to know the real catch to all this? When you show up for yourself, you just might find out that the thing you didn't feel like doing, or that you were afraid to do, you actually enjoy. Maybe even love!

For a very long time, I would tiptoe around working out. There were reasons, of course. One, I didn't grow up in a family that made fitness a priority. My mom was always on a diet of some sort, and she would walk for exercise, but that was it. I'd never really seen my dad work out. So when I started to not feel so great about my appearance, I thought, *Maybe I should work out.* But I was weary of doing anything strenuous because of my neck injury.

I went to see several different doctors about my neck and back, and more than one said, "Perhaps if you start working out and weight training a little bit, to strengthen the muscles in your neck and back, you may see some relief." And as much as that sounded like it could be helpful, in the back of my mind I was also afraid that I might hurt myself more. It's almost as if I was using my injury as an excuse to not show up for myself. I wouldn't even give myself the opportunity to see if it was going to work.

That went on for well over a year. Honey, I fought hard to not go to the gym. I was full of fear. I knew that on a regular day, a flare-up in my neck could have me stuck not being able to turn my head to one side for a week. What would happen if I actually made it worse? I didn't want to be out of commission any more than I had to be. But the words of the doctors kept eating at me. My own words to friends and family came back to haunt me. See, I was the first person to tell somebody how they could help themselves. And there I was, not showing up for me.

You ain't even going to at least try to see if this gym thing can work?

So I finally got a gym membership. I was always good with walking or running on the treadmill or using the elliptical. But the weight training was scary! It seemed too hard. And this is the God's honest truth: I was also afraid to look ridiculous. It's why I never took aerobics classes. It's why, beyond the fear of reinjury, I didn't go anywhere near the weights. I cared too much about what people thought. I didn't want them to say, "Lord, have mercy, this woman doesn't know what she is doing." I'd literally made up all these stories in my head of what other people would be thinking about me at the gym.

Honey, that was a whole mess. Because here's what I know now: There wasn't a single person in that gym thinking about me. I'd convinced myself these people were going to see me and say, "Oh, she's totally out of shape," when in reality, everyone in that space was dealing with their own issues and trying to reach their own goals. Underneath all my fear and hesitation was a deeper truth: I would rather stay in pain than do what I needed to do to heal. *oh yeah?*

Gratefully, something just clicked one day and I said to myself, *Girl, how much longer are you going to put yourself through this? How are you going to know if you don't even just try? Stop worrying about what the folks think about you.* I went to the gym, and I admit, the first two days made me super nervous. I did my normal treadmill and elliptical routine and then sat in the sauna for a while. I'd shown up. That was the first step.

Not too long after that, I started watching a couple of videos on YouTube that showed exercises for strengthening the neck and the back. I decided to just go for it. I would try those exercises the next time I went to the gym. I figured I didn't have anything to lose, and if somebody said something to me about doing it wrong, I'd just ask, "Well, can you help me do it right?"

But honey, no one was paying me a bit of attention. I did have one or two people come and say, "Do you want me to help you with such and such?" or "Do you want any tips . . . ?" but it was all in kindness. Eventually, weight training became something I actually love to do. See? There I was, having wasted almost two years being afraid of something, constantly talking myself out of it, when it turned out to be something I enjoy.

I did the same type of thing in my freshman year of high school. I'd been acting in church and school plays ever since I was a little girl. But in high school, there was only one drama teacher, and the rumor was that Ms. Fincher was the meanest teacher ever. I was so afraid to take her class. I listened to people around me who said, "Oh, you don't want to get her, she is so mean." And so I did not take her drama class—literally out of fear. Ninth grade passed. Then tenth grade passed, and I was still claiming that the class was too hard and the teacher was too mean. By eleventh grade, I had an English teacher named Ms. Clark who was also into drama. I started doing theater with her in the community, and one day she asked me, "Why are you not in Ms. Fincher's class taking acting?"

I said, "Well, you know her, she's not that pleasant. And she's hard."

Ms. Clark said, "Who said that?"

I started thinking about all the people who'd told me these bad things about her. None of them had ever actually taken the class.

Ms. Clark got me together, though.

"Tabitha, when you go out into the world, there are going to be a lot of hard things you're going to go through. And you're not going to have a choice not to take it. Not to like the 'class.' Why not start now with figuring out how to get past something that you're fearful of? Ms. Fincher is an amazing teacher. She's tough because this is her craft and she's very serious about it."

I took Ms. Fincher's class in my senior year, and it was the best class I'd ever taken. She taught me so much. Ms. Fincher was so cool, and she loved me, as I did her. I couldn't believe I'd lost the opportunity to study with her earlier in those three years of high school. I'd been taking classes and doing community theater outside of school when I could have been going to school every day and getting some amazing acting instruction. All because I thought it was too hard. All because I allowed myself to be influenced by people who didn't know what they were talking about.

People who have never done the thing you're aspiring to do should rarely be able to influence you or your decisions. How do they know what's right or wrong for you? Honey, they don't. They have no idea.

When I recently started my online businesses, I had to wade through my own anxiety and other people's opinions about me doing it. I had to say to myself, *Girl, if you don't start, you ain't never going to learn.* So I learned to stop running from things. I'm human so I do take a moment to feel what I feel, but then I move forward anyhow. After doing that enough times, there is now very little I'm afraid to try. I want that for you, too.

Listen, just start, baby. I firmly believe that if God places something in your spirit and you think of it more than twice in a day, you're supposed to do something with it. What a wonderful way to live life!

14

MIND YOUR
BUSINESS
WITH LOVE

*"Challenges make you discover things
about yourself that you never really knew."*

—CICELY TYSON

In March 2020, my son was diagnosed with motor tics. When it first started, we noticed that he kept stretching his eyes and jerking his head a little bit. It was literally around the exact same time that COVID-19 hit the United States, and he was having fevers and just wasn't feeling well overall. One day, he threw up at school and we had to go pick him up. I had already planned to make him a doctor's appointment to check out his eye movements and jerking, so I told Chance, "I'm going to take him to the doctor anyway. Because he's running this little fever, and I want to make sure he doesn't have no virus or whatever." I wasn't exactly thinking about the coronavirus, I was just thinking, *Oh, he must've picked up a bug from somewhere, and while I'm there, I'm going to ask about the eye jerking.*

Going to the doctor, my heart was racing. I'd already looked up his symptoms online and read about a couple of different possibilities, but I was still unfamiliar with it all. We'd never dealt with something like this before. When you see your child doing something that is not their norm and you can't control it, it can send you into a little bit of a panic mode—even if the child isn't complaining about it. It was upsetting.

So I shared with the doctor what we had noticed, and as I started to get really into talking about it, she silenced me. "Wait one minute, please." Apparently, she'd noticed it, too. Queston was sitting there reading a book, not really paying attention to us. Finally, she said, "Quest, I'm going to step outside and talk to your mom for a second, okay?"

"Okay," he said.

Now I'm really nervous.

"What you are seeing is called motor tics," the doctor said. She went on to explain what motor tics are, and that some children have them starting around six or seven years old, but usually by the time they're teens, they grow out of it. Definitely before adulthood. Sometimes tics can be caused by genetics, and sometimes it could just be from anxiety. There is no real reason or source that can be iden-tified; it just happens to a lot of children.

We knew nothing about this. No one in our families—that we knew of, anyway—had any record of it happening. So when she explained it, I instantly thought, *Oh my God, there's something wrong with his nervous system.* I started blaming myself. *It's because I suffer from anxiety.* Then the doctor said, "Listen, I brought you out here in the hallway because it always affects others more than it affects the person who's going through it. Has he complained about it?"

"No, he hasn't," I said.

"Right. Because it's not bothering him. It's bothering *you.*"

She went on with a word of advice: "We have to be care-ful about bringing it up. If he doesn't bring it up, you don't bring it up. I understand it's hard to watch, but the more you bring attention to it, the worse it can make it. So the best thing you could do is to ignore it, however hard that may be."

By this time, Chance had walked into the office, having come from work. The doctor shared with him what she'd told me.

"Try not to overreact," she said. "He is going to be fine. It's nothing major and there's no reason to medicate. Just allow it to take its course and don't let it cause any anxiety in you."

Honey, that thing hurt my heart. As a parent, seeing him not being himself was so hard. Chance and I both cried. We were just overwhelmed with emotion, but were now being asked to pull it together and act like nothing was wrong.

But that's what we did. We watched these tics come and go. When Queston is super excited or a bit anxious they come even more often. And I still wish I could make them stop. They're not painful or uncomfortable to him, just us parents. Queston never complains about them.

And it's only now, even as I write this, that I realize there is a lesson to be learned from this experience. There will be times when we'll see someone going through something, and for whatever reason, they are living with it just fine, but we think we're supposed to bring attention to it. We think we're supposed to make a big deal out of it, but we do that because *we're* agitated by whatever's happening, not them. And in doing so, we run the risk of forever changing how they see themselves. Now we have them thinking something is wrong.

Honey, when it comes to grown folks, sometimes it's just good to mind our business in the most loving way possible. How someone who is a full-fledged adult lives their life is just not our business. Sometimes the things that happen to them are not our business. Even if we see it, even if we notice it, if it's not causing them harm or inflicting pain on others, then honey, sometimes it just ain't our business. We have to stop attaching ourselves to other people's problems. Sometimes we are actually creating a problem that wasn't there in the first place.

Because let me tell you what I know to be true. Had my husband and I ignored what the doctor said and instantly started catering to this thing and making it a big deal, it might have destroyed our child's confidence. It could have made him feel insecure. It could have silenced him and caused more harm than good. We had to make a choice, even though it was very difficult to watch as parents, to put aside what we thought was normal or perfect. We had to sit back and let our child be the human he is. This is his personality. This is his journey. There's a reason he's going through it. My job is to love him through the process, not bring it up all the time. To be a mama, as I always have been, and support him.

So I hope that if you're witnessing something happening in someone's life—not life-threatening or harmful things, but simple day-to-day choices and experiences—and it's killing you inside not to say something, let this story be a little reminder to ask yourself, *If I bring attention to whatever this thing is, am I going to help the person or am I going to hurt the person?* And if you know for certain, without a shadow of doubt, that there's nothing you can do to help in that moment, then maybe don't say anything at all. Maybe continue to love them just as they are, and let whatever it is pass. And if it doesn't pass, let it be. Because that's part of who they are and how they're supposed to be. You mind your business and be okay with it.

PICO DE GALLO–STUFFED AVOCADOS

I love avocado. I love pico de gallo. If you put them together, it's really guacamole, but honey, when I'm trying to act fancy, I just stuff the pico in the avocado and it's equally delicious. This is also a wonderful breakfast option, especially when you're trying to eat healthier and need something quick.

A ripe avocado
Pico de gallo
Fresh lime juice
Roasted garlic vegan parmesan

Start with a ripe avocado. Cut it in half and remove the pit.
Get some pico de gallo and stuff it into your avocado.
(Try my mango de gallo! Just flip to page 68.)
Get you a little lime juice and squirt some on top.
Sprinkle some roasted garlic vegan parmesan on top.
See how easy that is? Baby, you are ready to eat.

SECRETS MAKE
US ALL SICK

*"No person is your friend who demands
your silence or denies your right to grow."*

—ALICE WALKER

I understand why we do it. Some things are just so hard to deal with. And yet, we must. Honey, stop denying that *it* happened. Whatever *it* is. There are things that have happened in our families, things that broke us as children, relationships that we refuse to deal with to the extent that we deny they even occurred. I know I've been talking about the importance of facing your life quite a bit in this book, but it really is the way to live a life of freedom and peace. We have to address those hidden things in order to get our healing, baby. Acting like that thing never happened, even if it hurts, is not the way to live free. If anything, it keeps you even more bound. It stunts your growth. Open your mouth, honey. Tell your story. You never know whose chains you'll unlock by having the courage to tell your truth, and you may even unlock your own.

I know more than most how much our secrets keep us sick. I also know the power of releasing those hard stories. When I was fifteen years old, I was raped. As with most young girls, this wasn't some stranger jumping out from behind a bush and attacking me. This was someone I knew. Someone I thought I liked. Date rape is pervasive, especially when young men and boys aren't taught what consent means. I just know that I said, "No," but he didn't stop. I just lay there until it was over because I knew I couldn't fight him off.

For the longest time, I thought it was my fault. That I was responsible for what happened to me. There weren't many PSAs or the #MeToo movement back then. There wasn't the wealth of information about consent and accountability that we have now. I bought the lie that because I had snuck out of the house with my friends and gone to a party, somehow that meant I got what I deserved. I really thought, *That's what you get, Tab. You didn't have no business sneaking out of that house, and you had no business going to that party.* Like many young girls, I blamed myself.

So for nearly twenty-five years, I kept that secret. I never told a soul, not even Chance. Then one day I posted a live video on Facebook, and the story just poured out of me.

Now, y'all know I don't believe much happens by accident. There was likely someone who needed to hear my story right then. To know that they weren't alone. But it was also freeing for me. The weight had lifted. Of course, I knew by then that the only person responsible for rape is the rapist, and there is absolutely nothing a person can do to "cause" themselves to be raped, but still, opening up that day was healing for me.

The catalyst for me sharing that day was a devastating one. Prior to me posting that video, the guy who'd hurt me had sent me a friend request. I had not seen him since high school—I'd heard he went to prison for quite a few years—but apparently he was out and wanted to, I guess, keep in touch?

Baby, that fifteen-year-old girl living inside me froze in terror when she saw his name and little picture pop up on the screen. I became nauseous. I couldn't breathe. A searing pain shot through my tightening chest. Neither she nor I felt safe. The source of our trauma had returned.

It was in that moment that I realized just how much what he did to me was still holding me hostage. I didn't know how to feel. I couldn't believe something that had happened so long ago, something I thought I had tucked away and hidden from myself, was still very much present.

But that's how our triggers work, right? It only takes one small, seemingly insignificant thing—a voice, a tone, a picture, a smell—to provoke a reaction. Even if we've done healing, we can be triggered. Healing is continuous work. Seeing his friend request made me physically and emotionally sick. So much so that I sat quiet for a couple of days trying to process what I was feeling and why.

Then one particular day, I was stuck in traffic on the 405 freeway, and whenever I'm in a traffic jam I assume God has placed me there to have some alone time with Him. I turned my music down in my car and sat in silence. That's when I heard the words so clearly. God said, "Your secrets are making you sick."

It was like the wind was knocked out of me. I began to pray as I was driving. "God, why are you saying this to me?" I asked. The response came through, honey, so quick: "If your secrets, those things you kept buried inside for almost twenty-five years, could grab you and take control of you as sudden as they did, what other people are dealing with secrets that are making them sick?"

I'd just started doing videos and was very new to the whole YouTube/Facebook/Instagram thing. But I knew God was telling me that I needed to tell my story. I needed to tell my story *out loud*. I needed to release it! And honey, I did not want to. I'd never told my daddy. I didn't want him to feel responsible, like he didn't protect me the best he could. I'd never told my husband. I was so afraid he might look at me differently.

But I knew I could no longer be in denial about it happening. And I knew that this had come back up for a reason. It wasn't about him. It wasn't about what happened all those years ago. It was about what I still allowed the trauma to do to me because I had not released it; I had not released myself from the guilt and shame. Keeping it secret was my way of denying it. So on that very day, I made the decision to share my story on video. And my God, I think that was one of the first nights I realized my videos were changing people's lives. I received hundreds, if not thousands, of messages. Most said, "This was for me tonight. I've been keeping this a secret." They confessed to me the things they were holding. By sharing, I was helping people break their own cycles, walls, and curses. Folks were being pulled out of darkness. My story let them know that it was okay to not hide or feel shameful anymore.

And it was certainly a blessing for me. I needed to know it was okay for me to be free of this. Most important, I needed to know that it was not my fault. It didn't matter that I'd snuck out the house. It didn't matter that I'd gone to a party. It was never my fault that he chose to continue after I said no; that he chose not to stop. And the moment I realized that, the moment I stepped out of the denial and acknowledged that it had happened, the moment I talked to my husband and then spoke to the world, it was like a chain had been lifted off me. It's like I could breathe so much better. And I felt free of something I didn't even know was holding me.

Secrets have the ability to fester into tumors, cancers, panic attacks, anxiety—all types of ailments in the body. The things we keep inside, they grow. And sometimes, it's not until you're triggered by something that you realize it's there. *That's what's been making me sick?* Honey, I'm here to tell you . . . you deserve freedom from that thing. I don't care what your part in it was, if any. Holding the secret in your mind, heart, and body is making you mentally, emotionally, and maybe even physically sick. You deserve to be free from it. You owe that to yourself. You owe yourself the freedom so you can breathe again. So you can look at yourself in the mirror and be okay with who is looking back at you. Baby, it's time to release those secrets and get your freedom. You absolutely deserve it.

TSA

 When did we become people who choose to judge each other's every move? This is especially common on social media. When somebody posts something, another person will post a nasty or rude comment instead of looking to understand whatever it is the person is trying to say. This inclination to make the worst comment in order to get a reaction is dehumanizing, and it's time for it to stop.

And yes, it's happened to me, but I've seen people do this to so many. I've always wondered what it does for that person being cruel. How does it serve you to hurt others? What kind of satisfaction comes when you inflict pain? Perhaps you are hurting. I get that. Somebody may have hurt you so bad, and your way to feel better is to cast that out onto others. But surely it isn't taking that pain away. It isn't really making you feel better, right? Maybe it's time to simply deal with the source. Go to the root of your hurt so you can stop dumping your pain on people you don't know on the internet. I promise, it's not making you feel better. In fact, it's probably only making things worse.

We have hearts, which means we are designed to love, naturally. That's how God designed us. If, in your day-to-day life, you are intentionally trying to be mean to people, to inflict pain, then consider this announcement for you: Check yourself, honey. Whether you are on social media or out at the grocery store, ask yourself some questions. *Why am I doing this? What do I get out of making people feel bad? What is my intention at this moment? Am I leading with love? Or am I really trying to hurt somebody because I'm hurt? Do I have a reason to want to judge somebody or say nasty things or have an attitude?* Then decide to not do it anymore. Create an intention to love, and watch how it comes back to you.

VEGAN TUNA MELT

When I was younger, me and my cousin used to go to the club, honey. Afterward, we would go to Waffle House, and I always got a tuna melt. They were so good! So when I have that urge for my vegan tuna melt, the thought that comes to my spirit is all the fun we had, laughing and recapping our night of dancing.

A can of hearts of palm

Dill (fresh or dried)

Any onion and herb seasoning

Old Bay seasoning

Smoked paprika

Garlic powder

Black pepper

Roasted seaweed (nori), in large or small sheets

Vegenaise (vegan mayo)

Sweet relish

Dijon mustard

Purple (red) onion, minced

Whole wheat or sprouted bread (*I love Dave's Killer Bread*)

Vegan butter

Vegan cheese

A pickle, if you like

Put the hearts of palm in your food processor. Pulse it just enough so it has that tuna-ish consistency. Make sure you don't overprocess it.

Add the chopped hearts of palm to your pan.

Then, a little dill.

Some onion and herb seasoning.

A little Old Bay.

Some smoked paprika.

A little garlic powder, or a whole lot, because that's your business.

A little black pepper.

Crumble a little roasted seaweed into the pan.

Look at you not needing measurements and things. Cooking by the spirit is the only way, honey.

Mix everything together and sauté on medium to high heat until the mixture turns a light brown. Remove it from the stove and set it aside to cool for a little bit.

In a bowl, mix up some vegan mayo, a little sweet relish, a dab of mustard, and a little onion.

Grab your bread and add just a little vegan butter to both sides.

Lay your cheese on the bread, spread your heart of palm mixture on top, and cover it with another slice of bread.

Grill it on medium heat, and if it takes too long to brown, gently increase the heat.

Flip it and grill the other side.

Place it on your plate, with a pickle, if you like, because that's your business.

Ooh, God, we thank you. Enjoy!

STRONG AND WRONG

"You're not obligated to win.
You're obligated to keep trying to do the
best you can every day."

—MARIAN WRIGHT EDELMAN

Have you ever felt so strongly about something that every fiber of your being said it was true, and then you learn that you are 1,000 percent wrong? Whew! I know how that feels. But let me help you with it. Nobody can tell you how to feel, okay? Know that. But you can feel strongly about something and still be wrong. Yes, your feelings are valid. They are. But just because your feelings are valid doesn't mean the way you express those feelings is always right.

It is so important that we recognize the difference between being right and just being caught up in our feelings.

Sometimes we have to step back from a situation and say to ourselves, *Am I just caught up in my feelings, or am I right? Everybody is saying I'm wrong about this. Maybe I am?* You can feel however you want to feel, baby. But that does not make you right, and you have to be okay with that.

When I was growing up, I thought my family was like the Cosbys. Every Thursday night at eight we'd sit down as a family and watch *The Cosby Show* and I'd think, *Yeah, that's us; we're perfect just like Cliff, Clair, Sandra, Denise, Vanessa, Theo, and Rudy.* Part of the reason I believed this was that my parents never argued in front of us. They never let us know how bad things actually were between them. But then Halloween 1992 came, and my parents separated. I was in eighth grade, and I was so hurt. My perfect picture of our family was shattered, and the devastation was incredibly hard. They would later divorce, and just as I'd begun to wrap my mind around them never being together again, my father remarried. I was in eleventh grade by then, and angry. I felt like my stepmother was the reason my parents had separated, and I held a grudge against her for the longest time.

With all the anger I was holding inside, I needed a place to put it. As a daddy's girl, I could never be mad at my daddy, right? I certainly wasn't going to lash out at my mother. I needed a person to blame for the destruction of my perfect family. The new woman who had entered our lives was the perfect candidate. That's what humans do sometimes, right? We find someone to blame when we are hurt instead of trying to understand the situation.

But honey, then I grew up. And got married. And began to have challenges in my own marriage. Troubles that could have easily led to divorce if we hadn't chosen to stay together and work it out. And that's when I got a clue. As a child, it's impossible to understand what we call "grown folks' business." At thirteen or fifteen, you don't understand what it takes to maintain a healthy and happy marriage. And you shouldn't understand it, baby, because you are a child. It's usually once you begin your own relationship journey that you have to stop and say, "Yes, I was angry. Yes, that made me sad. But yes, I was wrong."

I was wrong to hold a grudge against my stepmother for as long as I did. I was in my thirties by the time I finally woke up one day and thought, *Now, Tab, wait a minute. This ain't ever been about her.*

My parents were just not happy with each other anymore. They were two human beings predestined to come together to create my sister and me. To be the vessels through which we came into this world. But then they grew apart. Maybe we were the only reason they were ever together. Maybe it was God's intention all along for them to *not* stay together forever. Maybe they weren't meant to grow old together and be married forever. Maybe they were simply together in order to bring forth me and my sister and to establish great character in both of us, because they raised us with what we needed to navigate this world. I don't know, honey. But what I do know? My stepmom did not deserve the years of side-eyes I gave her and grudges I held against her. I was never overtly disrespectful, but I would never allow her to get close to me.

I had to apologize.

I ended up doing a video with her and my dad where I apologized to her for being a young girl who did not understand what marriage and relationships were all about and who had wrongfully judged her. I said, "I am so sorry if I ever gave you a hard time or made you uncomfortable, because it had nothing to do with you. Your relationship with my father, and my mother's relationship with my father, were simply not my business." She accepted my apology with tears and love. She also apologized right back to me for feeling the same way. It was such a beautiful moment of love and acceptance.

My parents were certainly my whole life as a child. But how they lived their lives and the choices they made were none of my business. I had to understand that although my feelings of separation and frustration and longing were valid, I was very wrong in how I expressed them. I didn't take the time to learn about this woman. I didn't take my time to grow up before I made a judgment call. I was wrong, and I had to be okay with that.

Being okay with being wrong is powerful all in itself. It means that you have learned. That you're growing. This experience also made me respect my own relationship with Chance even more. I wasted so much time believing some story, some narrative that I had created in my head about my stepmother. And at the end of it all, she is one of the best things that ever happened to my daddy. She cares for him. Takes care of him. She loves him just endlessly. And now, after I worked through my stuff, we are such good friends.

Sometimes we'll feel so strongly about someone without ever knowing the truth, without ever having a conversation with them, without ever telling them how we truly feel. We will go months and months, maybe even years, missing out on opportunities to grow in a relationship with someone, or even with the people adjacent to the situation. I know my "strong" feelings put a strain on me and my dad sometimes. My dad would try to please me and try to please her at the same time. I could have easily prevented all that by taking the time to understand.

Today, because I don't have those issues with my step-mother anymore, my daddy doesn't have to do a dance whenever we are both in the room. He doesn't have to be on one side—uncomfortable in his home, uncomfortable in his marriage. We're now all on the same page.

Honey, let me say it again: Nobody can tell you how to feel. Whatever you feel or felt, especially as a child, should be honored. But your feelings won't always make you right in a situation. Take a minute to get still. Look for the source of your emotions. Get to the root of the issue. Deal with whatever you believe the situation says about you (which is usually why our feelings are so strong in these scenarios). Then acknowledge what you're feeling and find an honest way of dealing with it. That way, you can really start to understand the whole situation—not just your feelings, but those of the other people involved. Very good?

TSA

Some folks love to blame everyone or anyone they can. And then one day, they run out of folk to blame. It's easier to blame someone, though, right? It's easier to be mad. It's easier to point the finger at everyone except ourselves. But think about this: If the person you are blaming truly did something to you that caused you hurt and pain, how is blaming them going to heal you? What makes you think that holding on to it is going to make you feel any better? That's right. It won't.

So let's stop playing the blame game. Let's focus on doing the work to heal ourselves. No, it doesn't let the person "off the hook." It actually just takes our attention away from them and places it onto ourselves. Don't let a person or circumstance hold you hostage in the blame prison.

You heard me, baby. Blame is a prison that gives the illusion of freedom—you think you feel better about what happened or where you are—but really, you are bound in your misery. Get out of the blame game, baby. Look yourself in that mirror and say, "No more." Yes, they did that thing. But despite it all, you're still here. Only you can control how you move forward. Blaming them is never going to help you get unstuck.

WE ALL HAVE VALUE

*"My mission in life is not merely to survive,
but to thrive; and to do so with some
passion, some compassion, some humor,
and some style."*

—MAYA ANGELOU

We were blessed to move into a new home in a beautiful new neighborhood not too long ago. I love it dearly, and although the new home is not far from where we lived before, a few blocks makes a huge difference.

Establishing relationships with our neighbors has been a bit challenging sometimes, though. At our old house, our neighbors were very nice but mostly stuck to themselves. We'd wave and maybe have small talk but nothing intimate. This was very different from our time in Baldwin Hills, where we lived when we first came to LA and where we knew and talked to our neighbors all the time. And it was completely different coming from North Carolina, where everyone on your block feels like family. Nevertheless, I was so excited about our new place and looked forward to hopefully establishing relationships with at least the people who lived in our same cul-de-sac.

One day, I was working on a show at our home with a camera crew of three people. In one scene, Queston and I were walking our dog, Blacky, right in front of our home. When the camera panned, there was a man, our neighbor, standing outside his home with his hands on his hips. He looked angry. Being Tab, I said, "Hello there! How you doing?" He didn't say anything. At first I thought he didn't hear me. "How are you doing?" I repeated.

Honey, this man, easily in his sixties, grimaced and then rolled his eyes. The look on his face was so rude and nasty. It was clear he was not happy about our presence. Then he got into his car, which was parked on the street, and shot us another glare, as if we were going to mess with his car.

We weren't making any commotion. We were in front of our property, clearly nowhere near his car. But there he was, shaking his head in disgust. I thought I was going to get an opportunity to meet a new neighbor, and he just busted my bubble.

This wasn't the first time we'd gotten the cold shoulder since we moved in. Chance was walking near our home with the electrician when a woman dressed in her fitness clothes came walking by. He excitedly spoke to the woman, saying, "Hey, how are you doing?" and the woman looked at him like he'd just said, "Empty your pockets and give me all your money." She then took a deep breath, picked up her pace, and walked to the other side of the street.

Now, Chance and I are different when it comes to these kinds of blatant encounters with racism. He laughs at the ignorance and decides to not give the person any more of his energy. But it makes me so sad. Not in an "Oh, I can't function because this happened" kind of way. Honey, that would never happen. It just saddens me because we're still living in a world where a person can't move to a nice neighborhood and be welcomed by everyone, no matter how they look or where they come from.

So we've decided to focus on the neighbors who have been wonderful. The ones who sent us a lovely letter in our mailbox introducing themselves and giving us their number, and others who have been so kind since we moved in.

And shifting our focus is probably best, according to Chance: "There is a truth about this country and about this world that we can't ignore. I am no longer looking for people's acceptance. I'm not here to make you comfortable. We are good people. And if they act like that, they don't deserve my good heart."

Honey, Chance doesn't play those games at all.

But when I come across one of the ignorant ones? I'm still choosing to smile. I'm still going to speak.

Why?

Because I know who I am. I know I'm not the problem. We are here. We are raising our family here in this home and filling it with so much love. There is something within some people that's broken and scared, but I don't have to carry that.

And neither do you. Sometimes when good things are happening to you, something or someone else will come and try to steal your joy. They will try to make you see your blessing in a negative light. As if you aren't supposed to be where you are or have what you have. Don't let that devil win, honey. You are not the problem. Those negative things coming your way are sent to distract you from what God is doing in your life.

There is an enemy, and he has a job to seek out and destroy your dreams and your life, if possible. Don't you dare buy into it. Don't let anything stop you from growing.

And don't be like those neighbors when someone around you is growing and being blessed. Don't be upset that someone is promoted at your job, or gets married. If someone is blessed to move into your neighborhood, don't look at them like they are going to devalue you or your property. See them as humans who are going to bring you value. Know that we all bring value wherever we go. Yes, you bring value, honey!

WE'RE BETTER TOGETHER

"Even if a unity of faith is not possible,
a unity of love is."

—HANS URS VON BALTHASAR

I grew up in the church. Whether it was going to my great-granddaddy John's church with my grandmother, or later to weekly service with my mom and dad, the church was a huge part of my life as a child. My granny's church denomination was Pentecostal, or as she called it, *Holiness.* Because of that, she didn't believe in women wearing pants. She couldn't get her ears pierced. It wasn't until she was much older that she gave in a little on some of those rules. She started wearing her little jogging pants, and for Christmas one year, she asked for some super-tiny, itty-bitty earrings in the shape of a cross and some very small diamond post earrings. I think she thought the Lord couldn't see them if they were really small. I used to say, "Granny, you know your ears are still pierced, though, right? The Lord can still see them even if they're small." She used to get so tickled by me.

But for the most part, Granny stuck close to those teachings. She was always talking about what we should or shouldn't do. What the word of God said about this thing or another. That's one of the reasons I loved my mama so much. She always provided some balance to all that hyper-religious talk. She countered those restrictive ways of living with an attitude that would have probably been considered progressive in our town. She'd always say, ["Baby, don't you ever focus on religion. Don't you get caught up in it.] You just get caught up in your relationship with God."

I think that's why I have the perspective I do now. I consider myself a spiritual person. And oh, how I love the Lord. I am a Christian. But I'm definitely not religious. I see how religion, particularly as an institution, has caused all kinds of separation between people who need each other.

This was never made clearer than when I was in the sixth grade and felt the Holy Spirit in my body for the first time. Mind you, growing up in the Holiness church my whole childhood, I was used to seeing people shouting and falling out in the Spirit. I'd be playing my tambourine next to my great-granddaddy John and just look at everyone being slain in the Spirit. I didn't know why it was happening. As a little kid, it was a common part of my experience, and yet I often wondered, *What in the world are they doing?* But

I never wanted to do all that shouting and carrying on myself. I didn't like the idea of not being in control.

When I was twelve, a year into my parents' return to faith, we all went to a revival at this little Baptist church in Ruffin, North Carolina. Me and my good friend Leander sat together as the choir sang and Reverend Duncan Spears preached. Me and Leander had promised each other that we wouldn't catch the Holy Ghost. My favorite cousin, Sonya, who always sat with us, had caught it one time, and it scared us both! So we were determined we would remain in control and not catch it. Thinking back on it, I literally laugh out loud at how we thought we could control the Holy Spirit.

Honey, the Spirit was high in that building! Everyone was shouting. Leander and I were both just looking around wide-eyed. "Oh, God," he said. I was scared. Everybody was getting the Holy Ghost, and I didn't want to. We'd made our promise to each other anyway.

Well, in one instant—literally in a blink of an eye—guess who was on the floor? I'd caught the Holy Spirit, y'all!

Yes, I know. There are folks who don't believe in all that. That's fine. If you've never been slain in the Spirit or that kind of thing was never a part of your world, I suppose it is hard to believe. But honey, I was all the way in. The Spirit of God took hold of me, and when I finally felt aware of my body, it felt like I was doing a slow jog in place. I remember my Aunt San and a few other people had formed a circle around me. I could hear them praying over me and cooling my little self off with fans.

When I finally came to, Leander had his arms folded. He

was too through with me. I went to sit back down beside him and he looked at me and said, "We promised we wasn't going to get it, Tab!"

"I didn't mean to get it! I don't even know what happened. It just jumped on me."

I'm not going to lie to you, though. I was so happy about catching the Spirit for the first time. And honey, you know who I couldn't wait to tell about it? Yep. My granny! Everybody at my granny's church caught the Holy Ghost, so I just knew she'd be happy with me.

The revival had been on a Wednesday, so I had to wait until the weekend to see my granny and tell her about my experience. Now that my mom and dad were going to church, too, we'd all meet at Granny's house on Sunday morning before service to eat breakfast. She'd have some fried apples, homemade biscuits, and fried chicken waiting for us. Tab wasn't vegan back then, honey.

When we got to Granny's house that Sunday, I felt like my heart was going to burst.

"Granny! Granny!"

"What?" she said.

"I got the Holy Ghost!"

"You did?! When did you get the Holy Ghost?"

"I got it at revival on Wednesday night."

She said, "Where was this revival now?"

"At Shiloh Baptist!"

Granny shook her head. "Shiloh Baptist? Oh, you ain't got no Holy Ghost at no Baptist church. They got carpet in there? If it's no hardwood floors in there, you ain't got no Holy Ghost."

"No, Granny! I'm telling you, I felt it."

She still shook her head.

"No, no. I don't know what you felt. You were probably in there playing. But the Holy Ghost ain't down in no Baptist church."

And that was that.

I don't know what I felt hearing her say that. At twelve, I didn't know anything about the theological difference between the Holiness and Baptist churches. All I knew was that it had happened to me. I was there. I was in it. I knew the Spirit came over and into me. I didn't have to know anything else.

Here's the thing. We are all different, right? Whatever your religion or denomination may be, your walk with God is yours alone to have. The religious titles and various doctrines all cause us to break off into groups. We have the Baptists over here. The Holiness over there. The Methodist, Presbyterian, and Catholic squads on one side. The Buddhists on another. I could go on and on, but you get the picture. We're all spiritual beings, right? And as spiritual beings having a human experience, we're all connected. So why do we create ways to divide us? Whether we want to believe it or not, there is but one Creator. There is something or someone out there bigger than all of us. So no matter what title you claim for your Creator, know that we are all the same beings sent here on a spiritual journey together.

My granny shot me down so quick because that's all she knew. I'm grateful for the foundation of worship and praise she gave me, but I'm glad my mama gave me a different kind of teaching to go along with it. And yes, honey, I caught the Holy Spirit many times after that. Sometimes in a Baptist church. Other times in a Pentecostal church. And a time or two right there in my home, because that's my business. I was tearing the floor up with my shout at twelve, and I will tear it up now, especially if I have on my mama's shouting heels.

You got special heels for church shouting, Tab?

Yes, baby. I sure do.

My mama loved her some high heels when she was living. She had one pair she called her shouting shoes. They were her first designer pair—some Stuart Weitzmans. And they were leopard print. Oh, she loved them shoes. Right before she passed, she told me that she wanted me to have them. I was so grateful.

After she passed away, I wore those heels with jeans or my favorite dresses whenever I'd go out. But then one day, I wore them things to church. I couldn't even sit down. The shoes had me cutting up as soon as I got in there. I nearly tore the pew up, shouting in those shoes. I said to myself, *Oh, Moma is still in these shoes.* And every single time I wore those shoes to church after that, I would get to shouting. *Now, Moma, you are going to let me sit down sometime, if I feel like it.* Listen, baby. Moma's shoes didn't care if I was in a Baptist church or not, and neither do I.

And sometimes these divides we create extend outside

of our denominational differences. Too many of us have the tendency to talk against or shun people who are not like us. We know that death and life are in the power of the tongue, and yet we use our words to put people who are different from us, or who don't believe the way we believe, in a kind of bondage. I've seen this happen, especially with the LGBTQIA+ community. Some families who have children or family members who are LGBTQIA+ have this notion that these beautiful humans are not okay and are constantly telling them that they are living in sin or going to hell, or that something is wrong with them. That is just not right.

I've met so many children and adults whose family have turned their backs on them for simply existing. People who have been rejected because of who they are, for being the way that God created them. Honey, just because someone is different from you does not make them wrong. It just simply makes them different. We are all different, and we should all be able to live our lives as we feel we were created to live it, without judgment, without hate being spewed at us, and without worry about whether a family member— someone who claims to love us—will turn on us. Turning your back on anyone is not an action rooted in love.

So I challenge you to take a minute and put yourself in that person's shoes. Have you ever been judged for being different? How did that make you feel? Then ask yourself, do you want to be responsible for making someone else feel that way? Consider your thought process and figure out what makes you feel like it's okay to judge someone in that way. Think about what's missing or broken in your life that makes you so quick to hurt someone. Is there some type of high you're getting from it? I know you think it's about holding to some religious belief and faith tradition, but I suspect it's so much deeper than that. The act of rejection and causing hurt to another human being is so far from what I believe we are here to do or how God has created us to be. He created us to love each other. To truly see each other, and live in community without hate and anger.

Let's all ask ourselves: Are we living in love? Are we trying to include everyone? No, I'm not saying you've got to be friends with everybody. Boundaries are a real and necessary thing. I am saying that if you enter a situation where someone is different from you, you don't have to be afraid of that. Your reaction doesn't have to be one of rejection and exclusion. They can be a value-add to your life. We often fear what we don't know or understand. But honey, something beautiful can happen when we take the time to get to know someone who is different from us. You just might learn something about yourself.

And maybe that's it. Maybe we're afraid to learn that there might be some things inside us that aren't so nice, and that's okay. I get that. But know that you weren't born with that thing. I don't believe any of us are born with hate. You were taught it, or you went through something that causes you to react out of that pain inside. But now you have the opportunity to unlearn some of those things that you were taught as a child, teen, or young adult. Release the ugliness that pain has caused. That unlearning can be hard, but it's also transformative. It will put you back on the track of doing what we were all created to do: love each other.

Yes, there are people who are different from you. From me. But at the end of the day, we are all one. If you believe in a higher power, then you believe that we are all made in the image of God. So even if someone looks different from you, acts different, or is different, if you see them as made in the image of God, it will be awful hard to spew hate at them. You will be inclined to spread love the way God intended us to. Remember, we were all born with a heart, because we have been designed to love.

Let's not allow any differences, religious or otherwise, to keep us away from each other. Let's make love our daily intent. We are all together in this world. We all have blood running through our veins. After all, love is a universal language. So I encourage you to take time to focus on your relationship with the Creator, if you want to, and I'll work on mine. Because that right there is all our business.

TSA

 This is a message to anyone who may have forgotten that there is no person alive without fault. For those of you who have gotten so caught up in religion that you have begun to think less of others, I hope this opens your heart.

God can use anybody to bring about a message. He can use the homeless person in the street. He can use that neighbor you don't even like. He can use your coworkers or your children. God can and will use anybody to reach you.

So keep your mind open, baby. Let us not be so quick to judge someone because they don't look the way you think a so-called good person should look like. Stop thinking people are useless to you when they just very well may be the blessing you've been waiting for all your life. But there you are, blocking the blessing. Perhaps talking bad about them. Shutting them out. Don't you know that you could be missing out? You better allow God to use the people He sends as a vessel, so you can get that word you've been praying and asking Him for.

Everybody isn't going to have the same beliefs as you. They aren't going to look like you, nor will they have had the same journey you've had. Be okay with that, okay? I read something the other day that really spoke to my spirit: "We are the future ancestors. Behave accordingly." Do you feel that? One day your children's children's children's children will look back and say, "My ancestors did this. I come from a long line of this." What are you leaving behind? How are you acting?

Work on your dash, honey. You know . . . that line between the year of your birth and the year of your death that shows up on the tombstone and in your obituary? Work on your dash and act accordingly. Listen to people who you may not normally want to listen to. Speak to folks. Be kind to people who are different from you. You never know who you may actually be encountering. We all entertain angels unaware.

VEGAN FRIED PEACHES AND BISCUITS

This recipe makes me think of my granny. On Sunday mornings, she would make fried apples and biscuits. But at certain times of the year, when peaches were in season, we would get a big box of them so she could preserve them. Of course, she let me eat them as we went. She never fried her peaches, though. Her thing was apples or pears. But one day I was thinking about her and thought, *You know what? I'm going to fry me some peaches and put them in some biscuits.* And baby, ooh, it worked out.

Peaches *(a little or a lot, peeled or not, because that's your business)*, pitted and chopped

Oil

Seasonings of your choice

Fresh lemon juice

Maple syrup

Canned vegan biscuits

Ground cinnamon

Vegan butter

Put a little bit of oil in a large skillet and turn the fire on medium.

Add your peaches.

Add your seasonings. *(I like Chef Carmen-Atlanta's Igotchu Peach Cobbler Seasoning. It has nutmeg and cinnamon already mixed perfectly. But you use what you have, okay?)*

Don't it smell good already? Ooh, God.

As the peaches are cooking, add a little fresh lemon juice.

Then a little bit of maple syrup.

When the peaches start browning, that's when you'll know they're pretty much done.

Cover them.

Turn the heat off and let them rest so they can be really soft.

Now, if baking is your ministry, go on ahead and make some biscuits from scratch. That said, I usually use canned vegan biscuits as a quick-and-easy alternative. (That's my business. Don't judge me.)

If you are moved to do so, sprinkle a little cinnamon on top of the biscuits before you pop them in the oven.

While the peaches and the biscuits are cooking, put some vegan butter in a little saucepan and add some cinnamon and more maple syrup.

Put it on low heat.

Stir.

Keep stirring.

This is what you're going to sprinkle on top of the biscuits when you take them out of the oven. If you want, you can add a little bit of lemon juice to the sauce as well.

Finally, stuff each biscuit with peaches, then take the butter and maple sauce and pour it all on top. Saturate it. Make sure you have a towel or napkin on hand for the sauce or your drool, whichever one.

Lord, have mercy. Can you get into it? I promise you, you will not be disappointed. Honey, this is breakfast, dessert, or a snack. Whenever you want to eat it, you can, because that's your business.

Part Four

LIKE SO,
LIKE THAT

19

FREEDOM IS KNOWING YOU'RE ENOUGH

"Embrace what makes you unique, even if it makes others uncomfortable."

—JANELLE MONÁE

Here's one of those hard pills, honey: Everybody ain't going to like you. I wish it wasn't true, but it is. Everybody ain't going to love or embrace or support you. We have to be okay with that, alright? How "everybody" feels doesn't matter, but you matter. What *you* feel matters.

Now, if you follow me on social media, you know that Donna is everything, you hear? Oh, Donna is my hair, in case you're wondering. She has her own personality. But here's the thing about Donna: She sheds naturally as she grows.

She sheds naturally as she grows.

That's a word for you, baby.

Sometimes as we grow, we will inevitably shed some folk naturally from our lives. But losing them isn't going to stunt your growth. Nope, not one single bit. You're going to keep growing. When I comb Donna, I always find hair that has shed in the comb. It's like the hair had no more purpose for my head. It would be foolish for me to try to force each one of those hairs back into my head, right? They would just keep falling out.

The same thing applies to our lives. When people shed naturally from our lives, don't try to force them back in. They've been removed for your growth. Be alright with it and continue on your path. In fact, when certain people come into your life, God will show you when they should be there and when they should not. You know the saying: People are in your life for a reason, season, or lifetime. Well, honey, some of us try our best to force folks to stay in winter when they should've been gone last spring. But your spirit knows when a person has outstayed their time in your life. Things start to become uncomfortable and just don't feel right. Then they start to show themselves.

Honey, pay attention when somebody shows you who they are. As Maya Angelou said, believe them the first time. If you are having second and third thoughts about someone, it's probably good to not have a fourth one. Let them be on their way. Chance shared with me something rapper and entrepreneur Nipsey Hussle once said, and it rings true: If your circle does not serve you or does not make you better, you ain't in a circle—you're in a cage.

Yes, it can be very hurtful when you sow into someone's life, when you love people hard and try to do right by them, and they take advantage of you. But use that pain to draw some lines and set some boundaries. Then trust that when God wants somebody out your life, He will kindly remove them, and you won't have to do anything. There won't be no need for malice and no need to act ugly. Just let God do His work, okay?

Most of the time, the releasing of these people is necessary for your growth. But we resist the shedding and releasing because we are people pleasers. We don't want anyone to be mad at us. We may have moved on ourselves, but we still want everyone to like and love us.

There have been many times in my life when I've had to decide to just be Tab. I needed to be authentically myself, and I did that. But there were other times when I lost my way and chose to make other folks feel comfortable instead. In my junior year of high school, I was very much a hippie. I was making my own clothes and thrift shopping all the time. I wore either corduroy or denim bell-bottoms every day, honey, and still wear them to this day. My mama would always call me her flower child. She'd say, "Girl, you were born in the wrong era."

People at school would tease me to no end.

"You look stupid. Why are you wearing that?"

"Oh, so you're trying to do you? You're looking crazy."

You name it, they said it. The meanest, most ignorant words were thrown my way. The Black kids were telling me, "Oh, you're dressing like hippie white people." But I just got it in my head that I didn't care. I liked it, so who cared what they thought?

This is how I'm going to dress, and this is how I'm going to be.

Since then, I've always maintained my own style when it comes to the way I dress. It was just something I embraced and enjoyed about myself early on. Even my love for earrings started when I was a very little girl. It was something I got from my mama. She wore earrings every day. That was just her thing. And I wanted to be exactly like her.

I remember being five or six when I got my ears pierced for the first time at a store in our local mall called Saslow's Jewelry. I also remember the pain. The woman took out that small plastic-and-metal gun and shot the post right into my lobe. I was beyond devastated, but only for about five seconds. When they handed me the mirror and I saw myself with those tiny posts, honey, I loved it instantly. My only other thought was, *Oh my God, these are small.* I wanted the big ones like my mama had. That day began my now close to forty-year love affair with earrings. Honey, I feel naked if I don't have them on. The only time I won't wear them is when I'm working out in the gym.

I wore those first little studs for a long time, until one Christmas, my mama gave me one of those sets that had different color hoops and balls. From that point on, earrings were my thing, too. Even though I was a tomboy, I'd still always have earrings on. I'd never go without them. And as I got older, the earrings got bigger and more fantastic.

By the time I was a teenager, my earrings had to be big. I had one pair, some hoops, that I found at the flea market that were big enough to fit around my neck. Honey, I used to love them. My daddy used to call them door knockers.

Sometimes I would wear my mama's earrings to school. I'd dress up in little suits and stuff, trying to look just like her. When I look back on it now, I realize just how much of a blessing it was to aspire to the standard of beauty she set for me. Even now, when I wear any of the earrings in my thousand-plus-pair collection, I look in the mirror and think of my mom.

I held on to this individuality well into adulthood. I was never interested in conforming to a mold that someone else created for me. But then, in the pursuit of my acting dream, I began to contort myself into the image I thought Hollywood wanted from me. Remember the diet pills? The body image issues? Yes, I lost my way there for a few seasons. Fear tainted my thoughts. Made me think I couldn't be successful being myself.

When I got sick in 2016, everything shifted. After a year and a half of illness, of being afraid of dying, I thought, *If I were to die being this Tabitha, would people know the real me? What will I leave behind? This person that I've created to make other people feel comfortable?* I did not want to do that. I promised myself that if God gave me another opportunity to grab hold of my dream, if He brought me through the pain, I was going to just be me. I was going to be exactly who He created me to be.

I said, "God, if you heal me, you can have me. I ain't going to try to do this life my way no more. I'm simply going to live my life the way you created me to live it. I am enough."

I'm not going to lie to you—even after I started eating vegan and my health shifted, I was scared. I was very afraid to start peeling off the layers and getting back to the core of who I was. But day by day, I stripped off all the stuff that wasn't me. And honey, no wonder I was so sick. Tab was being suffocated. The true me was being smothered by the false mask I was wearing. Layers of other people, other voices, and other personalities that I'd accumulated while seeking validation came off. All the ways I was trying to fit in and be accepted were released. No wonder I was exhausted. It was tiring being someone else. I'd had enough.

And to those who didn't like the new-old Tab, well, that wasn't my problem. It was never my job to make anybody else feel comfortable about my life. This is my life. Your life is yours.

The moment I decided to be my free self, don't you know I gained *more* respect? That's what they don't tell you. People come up to me all the time and say, "Oh my God, I'm so inspired by your freedom. It's so amazing to see. How do you do that?" Listen, everyone wants to be free. So when you walk in it, know that people will admire that. I saw people start to change all around me the moment I started walking in my truth. You don't do it for that reason, but it's good to be a blessing that way, too.

Chile, listen!

Honey, be your own person. No one can live for you. Choose freedom. Choose to be yourself no matter who likes it or who doesn't. You can still be loving to people. You can love people and still demand respect for yourself. Poet Nikki Giovanni said it best: "Deal with yourself as an individual worthy of respect, and make everyone else deal with you the same way."

Every day when I look in the mirror, I remind myself that I am enough. I say that to you right now. Despite what anybody may have to say to you or about you today, you are enough. Yesterday, you were enough. Today, you are enough. Tomorrow, you'll be enough. Forever, you're enough. Change the way you think, baby. Don't give control over your life, your self-perception, to people who have no business having that kind of power.

When I first started doing videos, I received so many negative comments about the way I speak. It was mind-blowing the amount of time these people spent inboxing such evil and hurtful things. They said I spoke like a slave, called me a country bumpkin, said I was ignorant—you name it, they said it! And there was a time when I might have hidden my accent because of those words. In fact, for many years I did. Working in corporate America and auditioning in Hollywood, I'd constantly contort myself to fit the picture other people had painted of what it meant to be acceptable. For a while there, my insecurities had me believing that I needed to change in order to be accepted.

But one day, I realized that I wasn't free. I'd chained myself to other people's expectations in order to make them comfortable. I thought, *How dare I hide my mama and daddy, my granny and granddaddy, my cousins, uncles, and aunts who show up in this voice? How dare I hide those beloved people who speak like me?* That's when I decided to not cover up my accent anymore—and I will never do it again. I'm from North Carolina and very proud of it. If a role requires it, I can certainly speak differently, in the same way another actor might cover their British accent. But I'm not going to do that in my everyday life. I'm free. So you might not be from the South—maybe you're from another country. Know this: Your accent is not a problem.

I had to learn that. And I relearn it every day. Why give someone control over how I talk just so they can feel comfortable? Why give someone control over how I do my hair just so they can like me or want to hire me? However I show up has to be enough. However you show up has to be enough. And if we aren't liked, if we aren't hired, then guess what? We are not meant to be in that space.

If you are supposed to be there—wherever "there" is—ain't nothing going to stop it. Not your voice, not your hair, not your weight. Okay? The only thing that matters is that you feel good about yourself; that you feel genuinely comfortable in your skin—not based on what society or some industry says you should look or feel like, either. That's what freedom feels like.

I choose to live a life of freedom because I deserve it. We all do. No man, woman, business, or company can tell Tab how to live because Tab is free. And you can be free, too. I promise you, the freedom to be you is the best gift you could ever give yourself.

Is it hard work? Absolutely. Because you have to also be mindful of your own changes and evolution. Who Tab was twenty years ago isn't the same as who I am now, in my most authentic state. So you do have to continue to learn more about who you are as you grow. We are changing and growing daily. But it's worth it.

Live free and watch your whole world change around you. The way people look at you will change. They will even start treating you differently. Why? Because they actually see you. There's an old saying that goes, "In a world where we could be anything, the best thing to be is yourself." It really does make a difference. Can I say it one more time? You are enough.

TSA — THIS!

We must stop telling our baby boys and young adult men—even our grown men—that they are not supposed to cry. I don't know who made up that rule, but it is a lie. Men need to release just like anybody else. It hurts me to hear things like "Stop acting like a little girl" or "Man up" directed at little boys. We must stop teaching that, because what ends up happening is these little boys start holding in all their emotion, frustration, and pain. Then they start to act out, because they haven't been able to release any of it. Their sadness and anger just sit inside them, and they don't know what to do with those feelings.

And honey, guess what? Too often, those little boys who are taught they shouldn't cry go on to become problematic men. "Why is he always mad?" "Be careful—he's quiet, but he'll blow his top after a while." Of course he will! He was never given permission to release in healthy ways.

I honestly think we'd have much less crime in the world if somebody taught men early on that it was okay to be human. That it's okay to cry if things don't feel good or if you're going through something. That it's okay to not be tough. I've even heard people stop their kids from crying when they've lost someone. "Suck it up. It's going to be alright." Really? Oh no, that's not fair. We must stop doing that to our young men.

Some of us are creating monsters inside these little boys. They grow up to be angry, dysfunctional men who don't know how to open up to women, don't know how to open up to men, and are afraid to be vulnerable. Let us stop destroying our little boys' emotional lives by preventing them from being able to express themselves. Tears aren't a sign of weakness. In fact, it takes courage to cry. It's the brave man who can shed tears.

If you identify as a boy or man, honey, don't you dare buy those lies. You are human. If you feel a certain way, baby, you deserve to express it. God gave us these amazing human bodies that do all types of things naturally in response to an emotion. If you try to fight against what it naturally does, what do you think that resistance is doing to your insides mentally and emotionally? Baby, if you keep fighting those natural emotions, rest assured they will eventually fight against you. So take your moment and don't feel no ways about it, okay? Don't you let nobody try to make you feel bad about showing your emotion. Don't you let nobody try to tell you to man up because you are shedding a tear for whatever the situation may be, okay?

I am the daughter of a great, amazing man. The wife of a great, amazing husband. The mother of a great, amazing son. As women, we see you. We are telling you it's okay. Let it out.

I love you for this!

TAKE YOUR TIME, DO IT RIGHT

"Adopt the pace of nature.
Her secret is patience."

—RALPH WALDO EMERSON

I know you want it really bad. That dream is burning in your heart and you are ready to do all the things. The problem is, you don't know what you're doing. You're off to the races but don't know anything about running.

Slow down, baby.

Do the research.

Ask questions.

It's okay to take your time.

This journey, this life, is not a sprint. Success is not a

sprint; it's a marathon. The culture tells you to rush. To hurry up and get it done, whatever it is. But Tab is telling you to take your time. Take a minute or more to figure out what you're doing. Get you a mentor. Watch some videos. Honey, read some books. Spend the time right now to get what you need, in order to see everything you've longed for come to pass.

Your dream is like your baby. When you first conceive, it's important to get through the first trimester. However, just like with an actual baby, if you try to give birth in that first trimester, you will likely lose the dream. And yes, a baby can be born in the second trimester, but the complications are high and survival rates are low. The best outcome is for the baby—and your dream—to develop to full term before delivery. Give that dream time to develop.

Know this: I'm not trying to discourage you. It's great that you are motivated. And sometimes spontaneity is necessary. Sometimes you will have to move quickly. But that generally doesn't happen in the very beginning, when you may not yet know what you're doing. There's a learning curve with everything. Be intentional. Calculate your moves. You will likely make fewer mistakes if you slow down a little bit and do it right. And there are plenty of mistakes to be made just in the normal course of growing and learning. So why add on mistakes made simply because you rushed? You're still going to get it done. But you'll be happier with the outcomes if you pace yourself.

The great thing about destiny is that it's always going to come to pass. Whether you go slow or fast, it's yours. So make the journey work for you. I've already shared with you how people call me an overnight success and how wrong that is. They say, "She just came out of nowhere and went viral," not knowing that I've spent the last twenty-three years investing in this career. My destiny was always mine. It was mine twenty-three years ago and it's mine today. My dreams have been living inside me ever since I was a child. But you know what facilitated them coming true? Me being willing to take the time and endure the bumps in the road to get here. Me taking the time to learn my craft. To study those who were doing what I wanted to do. In the midst of the hardships and loss, I would watch actors I admired and try to figure out how they were able to master a character.

When I was six years old, I'd watch Keshia Knight Pulliam playing Rudy on *The Cosby Show* and think, *I can do that.* I'd tap my mom and say, "Moma, I want to be Rudy's friend!"

And she'd say, "Oh, you want to be Rudy's friend?"

"No, not in real life, just on the TV!"

At six, I didn't know what it meant to be an actor. I just knew there was something I wanted when I saw what was happening on that screen with a little girl who looked a lot like me.

"Oh, you want to be an actor," Mom said. "That means being on TV. It's called being an actress," she explained. That was it! That's what I needed to know. I'd found my life's calling.

And you know the rest of the story by now. The ups and

downs. The first disastrous trip to California. The second trip, with hubby and baby girl in tow. The unpaid movie roles. The nine-to-five jobs. The acting classes. The on-the-job lessons on interviewing celebrities and producing television.

Remember my first gig with the Buster Brown show in North Carolina? Well, after that, I told myself, *I know how to do this!* And so I arrived in LA with that same attitude. *I got this.* The first celebrity interview I did in California was a red-carpet interview. Except there was no red carpet. I was actually behind the scenes at some nightclub. I'd met this guy named Zeke who asked me to be a host on his online channel. The platform was similar to Myspace, and my first interview was with the rapper Wale. He was very young at the time and had just hit the scene. No one knew him, but I was going to make the best of it. It was loud in the club and it was difficult to get my questions out, much less hear his answers.

Oh, it's a little bit different here in Hollywood. I'm going to have to adjust.

And that's what I did. I learned from that situation and adjusted to the new environment. By the time I was repre-senting a local LA magazine at a red-carpet premiere for *Keeping Up with the Kardashians*, a little background noise didn't bother me.

You see that, baby? Audition after audition. No after no. A few yeses I will forever be grateful for. A few music videos and theater productions. A few terrible movies. I didn't rush this thing. Did I want it to go faster? Did I want to land the role of a lifetime ten years ago? Of course I did. We all do, right? But when or if that doesn't happen, we get back to work. We keep running our race. We keep growing and learning. Don't ever sacrifice your soul. That's what rushing will push you to do sometimes. It will have you taking opportunities that go against everything you stand for and believe in. Don't do that. Keep working. Turn those ten, fifteen, or, yes, even twenty-three years into your overnight success story.

When you choose to take your time on your journey, you may find that the dream looks different than you imagined. It's still what you wanted. It's still a success. But you couldn't have ever pictured the shape and form of it. My success in entertainment took a completely different route than I ever thought it would. There was no TikTok when I was running from audition to audition. But it didn't matter. My earlier experiences informed what I would later do online.

The internet was an open door for the authentic Tab to shine. It's why I tell anyone who has a dream to pursue anything in the entertainment industry that if they are not using the internet, they aren't trying. I'm a witness to the fact that if you know who you are, and have a little bit of experience and a phone, there's a window of blessing and opportunity waiting for you. The internet is powerful. It will make folks think you just came out of nowhere. It will make twenty-three years of hard work look like two.

I was on the internet, looking at everything from acting techniques to YouTube workshops to build my digital media skills. Yes, there were times when I was frustrated. I'm human. But I was mostly patient, because I knew there was no such thing as too much information. I chose to spend my time figuring something else out while I was waiting for whatever break was mine to come. You know the saying: *Stay ready so you don't have to get ready.*

Now, let me stop you right here: Don't think for a second that it's just as simple as turning on your phone and doing something without an intention. The internet requires intention and consistency. Consistency is just like a habit, right? We all form good habits or bad habits, but most of the time when we form them, we do it without thinking. There isn't much intentionality there. You might hear people say, "She has a bad habit of doing that" or "Oh, that's such a good habit to have."

I remember growing up and hearing my daddy say, "When you wake up, turn around and make that bed up. Before you do anything else. Then go wash your face and brush your teeth." He emphasized the importance of doing these things the same way every morning until it became a habit, a way of life. From that, I learned that the only way to make something a habit is to consistently do it every day. If you do that thing—whatever it is—every day, it becomes your way of life. It becomes a habit that's hard to break.

So I brought that same approach to doing videos. Sure, God spoke to me and told me to do them. And no, I didn't want to. I don't know how many times I prayed, *God, why do you have me doing this?* It didn't make sense. But I'd made my promise to Him, and I wasn't backing out. And in order for me to form the habit, I had to be consistent. Intentionally so.

And, honey, the beautiful thing is, that consistency paid off. It turned so much into a habit that now I can't even go a day or two without thinking, *Oh, Lord, I need to post a video.* And by doing just that, so many of my dreams have come true.

So, yes, I felt the Spirit press me to do videos, but I also had to be intentional in my obedience to those nudges. And in the same way I didn't always feel like making up my bed when I was little, *wanting to* didn't matter. I woke up each day and did what I knew I had to do. I was consistent with content because that was my way of being obedient. I logged in and created content every single day for two years. No days off. I was driven by my passion but also by my obedience to God, who said that I was doing this for a purpose. God was trying to show me something, and in order for me to see, I had to do my part. My part was being consistent. God said do videos about food? Well, I'm going to do videos about food. God said use my life to inspire people? I'm going to do some inspirational videos. It's the consistency that paid off, right? And then as things started to happen, I was ready for those things. I knew how to capitalize on the opportunities because I had those twenty-plus years under my belt.

But as powerful as the internet is, it can't work without you. The real you. You still have to figure out what platforms work best and what content aligns with your vision

and personality. I've booked more projects and partnerships in the last three years than I ever did in those first
twenty, but those first twenty are the foundation for everything happening today. And none of it happened by copying
someone else. I brought to the internet the only thing I had:
Tabitha Bonita Brown.

Life gives you specific opportunities to learn if you pay
attention. Travel if you can afford to do so. If not, go to different places right there in your neighborhood. Do activities
that will encourage your brain to expand. I promise you,
honey, it will never go back to its original form. Put new
things in your brain, and it's going to take a lot to go back to
old ways of thinking and being. Those new things, that new
knowledge, will serve you well as you are waiting for your
dream to come true. And this doesn't just apply to entertainment. If you want to start your own business but you're
sitting around doing nothing to expand your knowledge,
then you're not setting yourself up for success. Become curi-
ous about the thing you want to do. See it everywhere. This
could simply mean watching the way a restaurant manages
its tables, or paying attention to the way a mechanic prior-
itizes cars while you're waiting for your oil change. That
extra knowledge is going to not only serve your dream, but
build your character, too. In other words, it's going to make
you a better, more open, and even a more empathic human.

*Well, I'm going to school, Tab. That's how I'm going to get
my knowledge.*

Great! That's one way to move toward your goals. Some
people choose to be trained through higher education, and

I think that's a wonderful thing. But understand that there are other options. You *can* take your education in your own hands. Ta-Nehisi Coates dropped out of college but spent hours in the library reading and studying his craft, and has become one of the best and most celebrated writers of a generation. Steve Jobs, the co-founder of Apple, didn't finish college either.

School is wonderful. Get your high school diploma, because you'll absolutely need that as a baseline for moving through life. Get that degree if you feel like that's the best place for you to grow in your calling. But know that you can own your education beyond school. In fact, whether you go to school or not, you should absolutely take ownership of your learning. And this will look different for each of us. For one person, that might be seeking out a mentor and/or becoming an apprentice. For others, it might mean developing themselves personally and spiritually so that they will have the character and emotional capacity to sustain their success.

Here's the thing about rushing the process. If I had decided that my success wasn't happening quick enough for me, then I would have quit and all the blessings of today and tomorrow would have found someone willing to wait. Baby, I was alright with waiting. Why? Because I knew it was coming. My dreams never lied to me. And that's what I want you to know. You won't mind working and waiting if you truly believe the dream is going to come true. You have to know that you know. You have to say to yourself, *I don't know when it's going to happen, but I know it's coming. So I'm*

FAITH

not going to rush it. It's so true that better things come to those who wait.

TSA

Honey, I need you to take a little soul medicine, alright? Very good.

Listen, stop getting into relationships you're not ready for. Whether these relationships are financial, business, or romantic, too many of us jump into partnerships ill-equipped and end up losing more than the relationship. It's like a boxing match. Fighters train for months and years before they get into the ring. If they don't do that, it shows. Big time. Without training, they get beat up pretty bad. So let's stop jumping into these situations for which we haven't trained.

Can we train ourselves to be a good partner in a relationship? A good business partner? Can we train ourselves to do better at managing our finances? Absolutely. Honey, you can always be the best version of yourself if you put the time in. But if you are getting into these relationships with whoever comes your way and still not developing yourself, you are going to fail every time. Focusing on readying yourself will also give you the discernment to recognize who might be the right partner in the first place. I don't want you to lose the fight, honey, so stay out of the ring until you're ready to be there.

TAKE YOUR HANDS OFF—LET IT GO!

DID I ALMOST CRY? (YUP.)

"You always had it in you to create miracles, but you forgot that it required you to do the opposite of what you are doing now."

—SHANNON L. ALDER

There are some things in our lives we just spend too much time on. It's time to let it go. I don't care what it is. If you're stressing over it, then you probably need to be still for a pair of seconds or maybe even part ways with it. You've been praying and worrying all at the same time, and that doesn't make much sense, does it? You've spent enough time on a situation that probably won't matter in the long run, alright?

Very good.

And here's the thing about time: It will not wait for you. You only have 24 hours in a day, 7 days in a week, and 365 days in a year. All the time you spent worrying about something you have no control over could have been spent working toward your dream. If the situation is not serving you, honey, let it go. Whatever they said, they can't take it back and you can't erase it. Don't waste your time on things that aren't serving you.

Remember the shedding? Well, that doesn't just apply to people. Yes, if your circle of friends and family are not adding value to your life, it is okay to remove yourself from the circle. But if that job, that television show, that news feed, or those boots aren't letting you live your best life, then let them go, too.

Oh, and to be clear, just because you let someone or something go doesn't make you better or worse than that thing or person. It just means that that thing or person isn't serving you the way you need them to. And that's okay.

I believe that every person, every place, and every season in our lives has a purpose. But sometimes we stay too long. And when we stay too long, we end up wasting time that was better spent on the thing God has for us up ahead.

I shared with you how there was a whole season of my life when I got caught up in what I saw other folks doing. In trying to pursue my dream, I locked in on the way Hollywood said I needed to look and sound. I wasted a good amount of time trying to adjust how I spoke to people in order to cover my accent. I exhausted myself trying to look like other people. *She wore her hair like that? Let me wear my hair like that. My skin is darker? Okay, I need to have this look.* Baby, this world will have you twisted and turned inside out to please it. And it's still never satisfied.

What does it mean to *look* Hollywood, anyway? Let me tell you: It's whatever people decide it is. So, guess who *looks* Hollywood now with an Afro and a little extra weight on her? Tab. Hollywood itself is a construct. It's something we just made up. "Oh, that's Hollywood." Oh, is it? Is it really Hollywood? Or is it just another manufactured image created to appeal to a particular audience?

I work in Hollywood, and I'm the only one walking around looking like me. I prefer it that way.

But before? I blew more time trying to be skinny. I worked out to be thin, never to be healthy. And my body eventually let me know just how that was working out for me. Now, don't get me wrong. It's okay to want to look good. But when the external supersedes the internal, you have a problem. If the *only* reason you are working out is to look better, that's a problem.

Whenever you find yourself focused on things that aren't suited for you or holding on to things you clearly need to let go, it's time to have an honest conversation with yourself.

Who am I trying to be?

Why do I resist being myself?

I'm claiming that I'm "doing me," but am I really?

Love yourself first. Then you can go out and give other people love. Then you will know how to be loved. That might be why your relationships don't work. Maybe every time you engage with someone, it fails because you don't love yourself. You can't teach them how to love you because you don't know what that even entails. What does it mean to love you? You might be feeling lonely and praying that God sends you a partner, a lover. Well, the way you get there is learning how to partner with yourself. Be your own lover. Get to know you. Figure out what you love and like, so when somebody comes around and they are potentially that special one, you'll be able to tell them what you need. If somebody asks you, "What you like to do?" and your answer is "I don't know," that's your sign.

You deserve to know yourself. You deserve to love on yourself. Take yourself out. If you feel good about being with you then you can trust that the right person or people will feel good around you. You'll also prevent yourself from falling for some foolishness. When you don't know yourself, or what you like, you'll fall for anything. We're not doing that anymore, okay?

After you figure out who you are and get those initial answers, I encourage you to bring them right back to the Source. Talk to God about what you are doing and how you are feeling. When I got sick, I realized I was truly tired of doing it my way. Once I surrendered my life, I had to figure out who Tabitha was again. If you feel like you don't know yourself, let's start getting to know you today. I want you to ask yourself a few more questions:

Who am I?
What do I like?
What do I love?

What do I really want?

What do I need?

Who did God intend me to be?

Now, this may take you some time to discover, but we're not rushing, right? Once you know who you are and what you want, you can let go of all that other stuff and move forward. And the beauty of it all is, you'll probably end up someplace way better than you ever could have imagined. The dreams I had for myself, honey, could have never added up to the dream God had for me. This life God has given me is far better than anything I could've ever conjured up myself.

A few years ago, I was a judge at a vegan chili cook-off. They asked all the judges to introduce ourselves and share how long we'd been a vegan. When they got to me, I realized that I'd been a vegan for just under a year. There I was, a vegan festival judge, and I hadn't been a vegan for long at all. Since then, I've been on panels with doctors and nutritionists. I've also been the keynote speaker—all because of my journey.

It's amazing how quick things can change in your life when you decide to embrace who you are and just let that other stuff go. There's something awesome about submitting your will to the Spirit and letting God guide your life. You're likely to find yourself in places and doing things you could have never imagined before. When I started doing the vegan videos, all I had was my word from God. I didn't think anyone was really going to watch. It was just important for me to release all the things that I'd allowed to hold me back and be obedient. The Spirit said do videos? Tab did videos. The Spirit said tell people what and how I ate once I went vegan? Tab told y'all what and how I ate.

And when I talk about my life changing, I'm not just talking about status. It's great that people support me and love me. I'm certainly not complaining about that. But that's just a bonus. The most important thing is that my heart has changed. By letting go of all that stuff that was holding me back and being obedient to the assignment God gave me, I not only received better health, but a better heart. My mind was clear, and I became even more open to the possibilities.

I was definitely a loving person before, but now I'm just open to love in a different way. I know that I can do more for people in this state than I ever could before. So, yes, I might sound like a broken record, but that's my business. I need you to know that whatever it is you want to do, whatever you've been thinking about, whatever is nudging your spirit, if you can't seem to shake it, dive into that thing. Figure that thing out, because there's a calling in your life, an assignment. If all you ever do is look at it but never fully embrace it, then it's never going to come to pass.

Honey, I'm of the belief that if you think about something related to a dream or vision more than twice in a day, you're probably supposed to do something with it. So, baby, it is time to move forward with that thing. Let that other stuff go. Let that fear and anxiety go.

Yes, you're going to have folks discourage you. They may say, "Girl, you can't do that," or "Man, you're crazy!" Let them say what they want. Even if they are family or friends. Let them talk. You figure your thing out, because life is too short. Do you want to die with that thing left inside you? Of course you don't.

I know it's scary, okay? Some of that fear has to do with our need to be in control. We think we know what's best for us. But sometimes we have to step back and say, "God, I trust you. I'm scared, but I'm trusting you." Some of the biggest moves you're ever going to make are the ones that scare you while you're making them. Even if your legs are trembling and your hands are shaking, keep going. I promise you, baby, there is light on the other side.

You woke up today, right? Touch your heart right now. Is it beating? Of course it is. God meant for you to be here today. We are burying people every day. Folks are leaving here. I honestly believe that no matter how young or old a person is when they leave this earth, their work was done. Every day we wake up means we still have work to do. You're still here, baby—so what are you going to do with that?

Sometimes we get so fixated on a situation or a particular outcome that we can't even pay attention to everything else in our lives that needs tending to. Our inability to let our hurts and worries go will blind us to the good that's all around. On a daily basis, check yourself, alright? You know Tab loves a mirror. We have to be willing to look at ourselves. Get in your mirror and have a conversation with yourself. Ask, *What are you worried about? Why are you letting these people have so much power over your life and your mind? Who are you mad at?*

Here's what I encourage you to do: Let go of all that noise in your mind and heart. Embrace the fact that you have a purpose on this earth, and it's time for you to figure it out and fulfill it. You've got somebody's life to change, starting with your own. I know life can be bittersweet. We all go through stuff. We all are fighting battles, seen and unseen. But let's not let the struggle win. Let the struggle go. At least you will be able to say, "Man, I went down swinging. I went down fighting. Honey, I was trying."

It's time to let go. Let's throw away all that's worn out and old. All our old ways. All the things we used to do that didn't serve us or our purpose. All the things that were our norm but have never evolved. It's time to live our best lives. Having lived through a pandemic, we know better than most that tomorrow is not promised. But forget tomorrow—the next minute isn't promised. Let's choose joy and love. Let's choose peace. And then once we've got it for ourselves, let's spread it around.

So, let go of trying to fit in.

Let go of trying to please other people over yourself.

You are an original creation. It's okay to be whoever God created you to be. There's nothing better than originality. When I let go of the old Tab, a weight was lifted. I thought, *You mean to tell me all these years I was trying to fit in, trying to look and be and talk like other people, I was keeping myself from being free?*

Yep!

It's so hard wearing that mask. It's hard putting on that let-me-be-somebody-else suit every day. I know, honey. You feel like you *have* to put on that other voice when you go to work. You *must* pull out your work voice when you're talking to your supervisor. What is that? No, whatever your voice is, it's good enough. I know what society says. I know what the culture demands. But at what point are we going to get off that ride? It's exhausting trying to be somebody else every day. So let us acknowledge that our true self is enough, and stop it. You'll probably be more productive that way. And you'll definitely feel free.

Freedom is doing whatever you feel naturally and being okay with it. It is simply saying what I've been writing about this whole time: I am enough. Baby, let that stuff go, alright? Then figure out who you are. Spend some time getting to know you. Find out what you do and don't like; what you do and don't want. What does freedom from other people's opinions and judgments even feel like for you? Get back *to* you so you can get what God has *for* you.

TSA

Do you know that you can be influenced to do great things? Yes? Do you also know that you can be influenced to do some not-so-great things? Yes. As an influencer, I know how easy it is for people to get so caught up in what they see Tab do that they forget they, too, have something to offer the world.

Let me share this with you: You can have some amazing mentors in your life. You can follow all the awesome influencers out there and they can certainly offer you guidance and inspiration in your decision-making and ideas. But you should never allow a person to influence you so much that you lose yourself in the process. Influence is just that: influence. It does not mean you have to be that person. It does not mean you have to do exactly what they've done. Your journey is unique to you.

MORE THAN ONE ROUTE TO A DESTINATION

"Whatever we believe about ourselves and our ability comes true for us."

—SUSAN L. TAYLOR

I'm just going to get straight to the point. Stop letting people convince you that the way you are doing something is wrong just because they did it another way. There are multiple routes to any destination. We are all different. We've lived different lives and seen different things. You might iron your shirt one way, and somebody else might do it another way. Guess what? You'll both end up with an ironed shirt, yes? If I take the freeway downtown and somebody else takes the surface streets, we will still end up in the same place. So if I have to say it a million times, I will: Don't buy into the whole "I have to talk this way, look this way, dress this way, read this book, watch this show" foolishness.

No, you don't.

Find your lane, baby. I've seen highways with six, sometimes eight lanes. If everyone is going the same way, then everyone is going to pick a lane and ride in it. Yes, depending on the lane chosen, some folks are going to get there a little bit quicker and some are going to take their time. But we're all on the same road. You don't have to do everything just like somebody else to be successful. Figure out your own way and be alright with getting off on a different exit, your exit. Don't watch other people and think that if you don't do it exactly like them, you're somehow failing. You're not. The failure is in trying to do something like someone else. Being your true, authentic self is the best way to win.

There are so many ways to do things. We've talked about tradition, and I know that some of us are still hung up on that. What we often don't consider is that, at one point in time, that tradition, that way of doing things, was new, too. Whoever created the traditional way of doing [fill in the blank] was an innovator. So what's stopping you from innovating, too? Create your own path. Do you. Not everybody is going to like it, but that's not your business.

My husband and I lived together before we got married. Where we're from, that's considered a no-no by the church folk.

"Y'all shacking up? Oh, the Lord ain't pleased."

But let's be clear: God still honors my marriage. God still

honors good hearts and the good things people do in the world, whether they align with tradition or not.

When I arrived in LA, I was told that Hollywood would not take you seriously if you started doing YouTube videos. Social media wasn't a thing yet, so back then they didn't understand or respect the reach of those they later called influencers. And that was part of my resistance to doing videos. Now, what if, knowing full well what God told me to do, I had decided not to do the videos? Where would I be now? All because somebody told me it wasn't the best route to becoming an actress? Well, honey, you probably wouldn't be reading this book.

So I'm a witness to the fact that you don't have to do everything the same. In fact, you might be the one who creates a new blueprint in your field or your family. But you'll never know that if you keep trying to do it the same way everybody has done it in the past. Don't you know that it's your freedom to do something your way?

Thank God for being different. Thank God your creative mind can allow you to explore and do things differently. Thank God you don't have to be one of those people who remain stuck in one way of doing things their entire life. You don't want to be one of those people. You deserve more than that.

I encourage you to do whatever that thing is you've been thinking about, even if you have an idea to do it differently. Create a new path and a new way, because that's freedom, and because that's your business.

SMOOTHIE BOWL

Smoothie bowls have been my favorite thing since moving to California. It was never something we had growing up down South. When I discovered them—my first was an açai bowl—I was like, "Oh, I don't know how to make an açai bowl, but I know how to make a smoothie and put the same toppings on top." It's such a fun little treat you can eat somewhere outside or even just a different place in your house. It just makes you feel like you're somewhere, even though you ain't.

Let's make a smoothie bowl, alright?

Almond milk

A banana

Some frozen blueberries, strawberries, peaches, and mango, oh my! *(sometimes they come in a blend)*

Shredded coconut

Ground flaxseed

Fresh strawberries

Chopped pecans

Maple syrup

Put the almond milk, banana, and frozen fruit in your blender and let it do its thing.

Pour your berry mix into a bowl.

Add some shredded coconut.

Then a bit of ground flaxseed, because that's our business.

Add some fresh-cut strawberries.

Some chopped pecans.

A little more coconut, if that's what you like.

Add some pure maple syrup on top.

My God, my God, do you see what you've done?

Now, this is the part of the recipe that might be a little

different than you're used to. You must take the smoothie bowl, hold it tight in your hands, and . . .

. . . go eat it outside.

Yes, you read that right.

Yes, that's part of the recipe.

Go on outside, if you can.

Or head over to the cutest place in your house, honey.

Laugh a little bit.

Have a little sassy attitude about yourself.

Don't you feel good?

WHAT YOU BELIEVE IS YOUR BUSINESS

*"Know in your heart that all things
are possible. We couldn't conceive of a
miracle if none had ever happened."*

—ATTRIBUTED TO LIBBIE FUDIM

About six to eight months before she passed away, my mama and I had a conversation about her death. We knew she was going to die, and it had begun to weigh on me. I said, "Moma, I don't know what I'm going to do when you're gone. You're my best friend. What am I going to do without you?"

Always wise, she responded with compassion and honesty.

"I thought the same thing when Granny died. But one

day I was at work, honey, and having one of the roughest days. When I went back to my desk and sat down, there was a nickel sitting on the edge of my desk."

I didn't know where Moma was going, but I was intrigued.

"For whatever reason, I was just so drawn to this nickel. I realized in that moment I felt the presence of my mom."

"Really?" I said.

"Yeah. And after that, whenever I'd have rough days or maybe just really good days when I was missing her, I would find a nickel."

I couldn't help but laugh. "So you think Granny is leaving you nickels?"

"I think so," she said.

"Well, if that's what you think, what will you leave me so I know you're around when you're gone?"

"You know what? I'll double it, and I'll leave you dimes."

We laughed so hard about that. "Well, Mom, I'm going to be looking for them dimes."

I never told anyone about me and Moma's conversation. It was one of those things I just pushed down into my heart and didn't think too much about afterward. Those eight months flew by, and my mother made her hard-fought transition. When we finally returned to Los Angeles after the funeral, nobody had been in our home for the two weeks we'd been in North Carolina. The first night, my husband and I went to get into bed and when we pulled the covers back, my bed was full of dimes—at least seven.

Honey!

Chance said, "Why do you have dimes in the bed?"

I said, "I don't have dimes in the bed. We haven't been here. Why would I have dimes in the bed?"

That's when it hit me. I remembered the conversation with my mother.

No, it couldn't be.

But how else did those dimes get in there?

"Chance, I want to tell you something." I finally told him about the conversation with Mom, and it scared him.

"Oh, that makes me nervous," he said. "Don't tell me no more."

I spent so much time that night trying to make sense of it all. I wanted to believe it was true, but I just didn't know how.

The next morning, I was in the kitchen cooking breakfast when Chance, who was in the shower, started screaming and yelling.

"Tab, come into the bathroom right now! Right now!"

I go into the bathroom and he can barely talk. He's pointing at the shower, and when I look over, the shower floor had about five or six dimes on it. My heart swelled. It was true. Moma was there.

Ever since Moma passed away, to this day I still find dimes everywhere I go. In my roughest times, there's a dime. In my happiest times, I find a dime. On days when I just need to be reminded that everything is going to be okay, I'll find a dime in the weirdest place or mixed into some mind-blowing situation. We do have angels. And we are given signs every now and then to remind us that we are being covered and protected. For me, it's dimes. For you, it might be something else. The key to it all? We have to believe.

Now, I know some of you are thinking, *No, Tab. That's too much. I don't know about all that.* And I understand. The supernatural can be scary when we don't embrace it. This may be against what you believe. That's fine, too. But honey, know that God speaks in myriad ways. I love the Lord. I love Jesus. I am a true believer of all things—including angels and the world above that we can't see. As the ol' church folks used to say, God is still in the miracle-working business. Miracles didn't stop when folks stopped writing the Bible. I don't believe that for one second. Miracles still happen every day on this earth. God has done and can do more than we could ever imagine.

But none of it matters anyway if you don't believe. You want your miracle? You want your version of the dimes? You want those unexpected blessings? Decide to believe what you call impossible. Watch what happens.

Don't let people convince you that what you believe is wrong. When God puts something in your heart, or you know without a shadow of a doubt that something has happened, trust that. Yes, there will be folks around you trying to convince you that you are crazy. Or they'll say it's the devil. They told Jesus the same thing, you know. He's healing people and working miracles and those daggone church folks claim he's doing it by the power of the devil. So if people did it to him, they'll do it to you.

Don't you give it any attention, though. Stick with what you believe. If you know you've prayed on that thing, you've asked God for confirmation, and He sends it to you, that's all that matters. Guard your miracle, message, or gift with your heart. Don't expect people to understand. This is your journey. Trust your journey, and even in the traumatic times, trust the miracles that help you move through it.

It can be easy to forget this when we're going through something that seems unbearable, but God is trusting us to get through it. He knows we're strong enough to endure. He may not have caused it, but He for sure has equipped us with all we need to survive it. If you're still able to see the light, no matter how dark it is, that's a blessing. If you're still grasping at hope and holding on to faith, you are on your way to the miracle. Honey, it might be hard to wake up sometimes, I know. And your flesh might get weak. Keep believing! That's how you keep your spirit strong. Let nobody tell you what to believe, alright? You know what's in your heart, because God put it there. Keep believing in your signs. Keep believing in your miracles. Keep knowing that your angels are with you.

TSA

 One of the major ways I deal with life interruptions is by quickly prioritizing the need when the interruption arises. I ask myself, *Is this an interruption that deserves my time?* Because if it is, then it's not an interruption, it's life that needs to happen. But if it's something that can truly wait, well, honey, it will wait. That distinction is so important, because we can't control the up and down, back and forth. And sometimes an interruption is a sign that something needs to be tended to. So if it requires my energy and time in order to make room for peace within, then I handle it as it comes. If not, then I continue on with what I'm presently doing.

Not every interruption deserves your time and energy. And honey, I know it takes a lot of time to get to a place where you can decide to say, "This is not worth my time. I will not allow this to be an interruption." But when you can do that, you'll find that you will move forward through life with much more ease.

Like I've said before, consistency is what drives success. It is what gives you what you need to get where you're going. Develop good habits, and things will just start to naturally fall into place because you are putting in the work. But always be mindful to measure the interruptions and distractions that will inevitably come, to see if they're even worth your time. And if they deserve your energy, then give it to them, but get right back on track once you're done. And if you are being consistent, then when that interruption comes, you will know how to handle it and get right back to doing what you were doing.

Part Five

VERY
GOOD

GRATEFUL, GRATEFUL, GRATEFUL

> *"'Thank you' is the best prayer*
> *that anyone could say."*
>
> —ALICE WALKER

I was standing on the balcony of a beautiful luxury home in View Park, Los Angeles, looking out at an amazing cityscape. As I stood there, preparing myself to host the TEDxCrenshaw event, my heart was filled with so much praise. Why? Because, honey, I could literally see my past from where I was standing. A seven-unit, blue Baldwin Hills apartment building with a white balcony stood directly across the street. Visible from my position on that balcony was the apartment where Chance, Choyce, and I lived for five years when we first moved to LA. We'd come a long way from our days in that space, not just in distance, but in life.

Because of the things I've been through in my life, I live in a state of gratitude. Honestly, I didn't think I'd be here to see these blessings. That's why I'm a firm believer in stopping to acknowledge the grace life gives us. It surely could have gone another way.

Even as I write this, in my office, in my new dream home, I am struck with just how good God is. In our other home, I had an office. It was just the couch. Now I'm sitting in a space I decorated myself with a beautiful gold chandelier, a pink-and-gold couch, and a gold-and-white desk with beautiful decorative chairs and a little side table with a mirror on it. All around me are pictures of me and/or my daughter on the covers of magazines and fan artwork from followers. And of course, there's my ring light. Still recording videos. Still sharing my heart.

But be clear: It's not about the stuff. The stuff is just a marker, a tangible representation of what I know God has done in my mind, heart, and body.

I come into my office often, even as we are in the process of moving into the rest of the house, because I have to acknowledge every single thing I see in here. There was a time when none of it existed. And honey, here's the thing: None of it was here because *I* wasn't here. None of what I see manifested right now in my life existed because I had not made it to *this* point in my inner life. It's all connected. The transformations on the inside always show up as transformations on the outside.

So, gratitude has to be something we practice on a daily basis. Take a minute and look around. No matter where you are, know that there was a previous stop on your journey that looked much different. Know that you could have been somewhere else or nowhere at all. God allowed me to walk through this life, with all its ups and downs, and I'm so thankful. I sowed my seeds and now I'm reaping a harvest I couldn't have imagined on my own. This office, this home, is mine. And it blows my mind every time I think about it.

My gratitude also comes from the fact that I know where we came from. I never want to make the mistake of getting too comfortable. With solely thinking, *Oh, this is what I'm supposed to have,* to the extent that, instead of being grateful, I am entitled. There is a way to grab hold of your blessings without acting like God owed you those blessings, yes? If you're going to get comfortable, baby, find comfort in your gratitude.

Yes, you do deserve the good things that happen in your life. Yes, you are supposed to be there. God chose you for the journey, and you've sown good seeds. But cradle all that deserving in humility. Never lose sight of where you came from; the distance between there and here is paved in life lessons that you should never let slip from your memory.

Sometimes, when people reach a certain level of success, they detach from the lessons that got them there. They go a bit numb to all the emotions that can come up when they look around and realize just how far they've come. Again, the awareness of their worthiness shifts into entitlement. I never want to *not* feel. If I stop feeling, if I go numb to my blessings, something is terribly wrong. Living in a constant state of gratitude means that I'm very much alive and I'm very much in touch with who my provider is. God opened the doors that allowed me to walk my prepared self through. I'm clear about that.

An attitude of gratitude has so many benefits. When you live with that mind-set, you will appreciate your family more. When God brings you from a completely different way of life into a new one, He often doesn't just bring you. He brings your entire family along. I get to see my husband not be completely stressed about working, bills, and finances like he used to be. I get to see who he is and what he can accomplish when he's free from those worries.

Ooh, God, I thank you!

I get to see my daughter, two years out of high school, living her dream of being a model without excess worry or frustration.

Ooh, God, I thank you!

I get to see my son have the kind of fun bedroom that Chance and I could have only imagined as children. His bed is shaped like a car. Video games and books everywhere. A basketball court outside.

Ooh, God, I thank you!

Even with our oldest daughter, my bonus baby, Ty-Leah, I get to see her pursue her dream of running track professionally. She has to pay for her training, and it fills my heart with joy to be able to tell her she can come back home and not pay rent on an apartment so she can use her money and time to focus on the thing she loves without the added stress.

Ooh, God, I thank you!

Your freedom, and the blessings that come from that, can set the folks around you free if you let it. It doesn't matter what step of the ladder you are standing on right now; it could have gone another way. You could be struggling now, but if you ate today, then you are doing better than a lot of people. Stand in that gratitude. Find something, anything, to thank God for, and watch how your heart's posture will elevate you.

Remember when I shared with you the time I told God that if He freed me from the pain, I'd give my life to Him? Well, my life as it currently stands is the other side of that promise. It's the faithfulness and obedience that have given me these blessings. God said, "I'm going to give you this because you've been faithful." How could I ever go numb to that? I'll stay thankful for it all until my last breath. Don't take your blessings for granted, baby. Like my daddy used to tell me, "As quick as you got it is as quick as it can be taken away." So while you have what you have, be grateful for every little thing. Gratitude means you can be trusted with God's favor. So the more thankful you are, the more blessings will come.

TSA

 Listen, there comes a time where you have to make your own decisions on how to celebrate your victories, okay? Whether it is a small victory or something huge that happened in your life, it's still your victory, right? Don't let people influence you or get in your head saying, "Man, that's it? You celebrating that? Don't celebrate too soon." Don't allow folks to get you to doubt your victories. If you feel good about it, if you've accomplished something you're proud of, then, baby, celebrate your moment. You go on ahead and do that, because that's your business!

You are the only person who knows how you feel. You are the one who worked hard for that thing. So, yes, you are the one who gets to make the decision when or how or whether you celebrate your victory. Honey, it brings that old church song to my spirit. *Victory is mine! Victory is mine! Victory today is mine! I told Satan, get thee behind. Victory today is mine.*

Honey, did you catch those words? Victory is yours. So when folks start trying to mess up your day by telling you that your joy isn't worth celebrating, tell them folks to get on behind you. You celebrate your victories because, guess what? That's your business.

LOBSTER MUSHROOM PASTA

Nobody misses lobster like I miss lobster. When I discovered lobster mushrooms, my life felt like I had got saved, okay? Like born again. It's mind-blowing how lobster mushrooms literally look and taste like lobster. If you can't get your hands on them—because they are seasonal and hard to find—you can opt for oyster mushrooms and season them the same way. Just know the texture and color won't be as close to lobster as the lobster mushrooms.

Vegetable broth

Lobster mushrooms, chopped

A little bit of chopped white onion *(but make sure it's chopped fine)*

Some diced tomatoes *(fresh or canned, that's your business)*

A salt-free multi-spice seasoning blend

A little bit of garlic powder, or chopped fresh garlic if you have some

Angel hair pasta *(or whatever pasta you want to, because that's your business)*

Salt, for the pasta

A little bit of virgin olive oil

A bit of vegan butter

A little bit of chopped kale

Vegan parmesan

Grab a bowl and add your broth, lobster mushrooms, and onion. Stir it a bit.

Add your tomatoes, garlic powder, and spice blend.

Pour everything into a pan and let it cook on medium heat for a bit. *(A bit is however long your spirit tells you to cook it.)*

When it comes to a gentle boil, let it do what it do for a pair of minutes or so.

Meanwhile, boil your noodles separately in water with

a sprinkle of salt and a dab of olive oil. You can also add garlic powder to the water, if garlic is your thing.

Once it boils, add some vegan butter to give the drained noodles more flavor.

Now grab your kale and add it to the lobster mushrooms that have been simmering. Stir your kale right on in, along with more of your spice blend, and let it cook down for 5 to 7 minutes or so.

Now drain your noodles and add them to your lobster mushroom pan.

Add a little vegan parmesan on top, and there you go.

Ain't it good?

25

LISTEN FOR
THE WISDOM

*"Remember the wisdom of your ancestors
in order to become wise."*

—AFRICAN PROVERB

If you are from anywhere near Eden, North Carolina—
including Reidsville or Draper—you probably had your
hair pressed or an outfit made by my great-great-Aunt Bett.
She passed away at ninety-three when I was in eleventh
grade, but she was such a huge part of my upbringing. She
helped raise me, and I learned so much from her.

Aunt Bett was deaf and mute. Had been my entire life.
Apparently, she'd gotten some kind of ear infection as a little girl, and because she was Black, the doctors who could

have helped her would not see her as a patient. She lost her hearing as a result. So the only words she could say as an adult were the words she knew at two. *Moma. Papa. Eat.* Mostly she had a sweet groan she'd do that communicated everything she wanted you to know. She couldn't hear, but she could feel everything. Her other senses seemed to be off the charts.

So y'all know Tab has a huge imagination, right? Always had it, even as a child. My Aunt Bett taught me everything there is to know about doing hair. She also taught me how to sew and crochet. Even gave me a dance lesson or three. So at one point, I got it in my mind that Aunt Bett could actually hear. I thought, *Aunt Bett messing with us. I know she can hear.* I'm not going to lie to you. I still wonder about it to this day.

Aunt Bett's beauty shop was in what we called "the old house." It was the first house my granddaddy had built on his property. He let my Aunt Bett, who was actually *his* aunt, stay there. That's where she did people's hair and made clothes. That's also where I spent most of my time when I was little. If I was visiting my granny, I'd just walk over to the old house and Aunt Bett would be sewing or watching her "stories"—soap operas—on a black-and-white TV. She watched everything on that little TV.

She knows what's going on with those stories. I know she can hear. I know she can.

I would try to test Aunt Bett all the time. To try to trick her into revealing this secret I thought she had. When I was eight, I stood at the screen door with my back turned so she couldn't see me or read my lips. I said, "Aunt Bett, I know you can hear. I promise I won't tell nobody. It will be just my and your secret."

But she kept on sewing.

I still believed she could hear, though. I felt like she'd do little things to let me know she could. Whenever something would happen on one of her programs, she'd make her little noise, "Ah. Hmmmm." But there was one day that just sealed my suspicions for me.

I was the youngest out of all my cousins on that side of the family. My sister, Tasha, was the oldest. In between were my cousins Kiesha and Shelina. Now, you know when the cousins got together, especially when a little one like me got to hang with the older ones, we were bound to get into some mess. That day, my sister and cousins were cussing and cutting up. So I thought, *You know what? I'm going to cuss, too.* Honey, I wanted to see how it would feel coming out of my mouth. So I was just out there trying to be grown, acting like the older kids, just cussing up a storm.

Later, when Moma came to pick us up, Aunt Bett came out on the porch and groaned, "Ah hmmmm." She pointed at me, then put her finger to her mouth and shook her head, saying, "Hmmmm." Now don't you ask me, because I don't know how my mama knew what Aunt Bett meant, but she did.

"Oh, you've been out here saying bad words, huh?"

"Moma, I didn't . . ."

Aunt Bett interrupted and moaned, "Mm. Mmmmm."

And of course, you know who got in trouble.

From that day on, I knew in my heart that Aunt Bett

could hear. How else would she know I was out there saying bad words on the porch? That made me more determined than ever to get Aunt Bett to talk to me. I was going to keep her secret.

During the week, she'd go to a place folks called "the site." It was like a community center for the elderly. They'd send a van around and take people to the site to play bingo or do arts and crafts. It was Aunt Bett's way of getting out and having fun. But I'd like to think she had the most fun with us on the weekends when she would spend the night with us if my mom and dad went out somewhere. In 1989, Marcia Griffiths released a remix of "Electric Boogie" (aka "The Electric Slide"), and Aunt Bett came to spend the night with us. Honey, when we turned the song on, she came in that kitchen and cut a whole rug. She started catching that beat and doing her neck roll. She was the best dancer I'd ever seen.

And once again, I was determined.

"Aunt Bett, you can tell me. You can hear, can't you? I promise I'm not going to tell nobody."

She just looked at me and smiled.

I tried again another day.

"Okay, Aunt Bett, I'm tired of asking you. I ain't going to ask you no more. I love you anyway, even if you don't trust me. I won't tell nobody." (I told y'all I was determined. This went on for years.)

On that day, Aunt Bett looked at me and smiled. Then, she winked.

Honey!

That was all the evidence I needed. In my spirit, I convinced myself that was her saying, *I can't tell you, but there you go.*

But here's the truth in this whole story: I didn't need to know. It wasn't my place to be in her business. And her capacity, the wisdom that she imparted to me my whole childhood, wasn't diminished a single bit by her deafness—no matter to what degree it actually existed in my imagination. I spent so much time trying to figure out if she was hiding a secret that I'm sure I missed out on some amazing opportunities in her presence as a kid. I now realize that sometimes we are just longing for an inside connection. I wanted something special between Aunt Bett and me, a secret for us to share. But we can't force that kind of thing. Our job is just to love people simply as they are. To accept whatever parts of themselves they give us access to.

But the larger lesson is this: Listen to the wisdom around, no matter what form it takes. I often think back now to all the great things my Aunt Bett taught me. For a long time, I did hair to make extra money off the strength of the gift she shared with me. When she taught me to crochet, I watched her create all kinds of things—some I didn't understand, like the Kleenex box covers with hats to match. And although I haven't done it in years, I'm pretty sure if I started back crocheting, I could pick it right on up. She taught me not to be a follower. I knew when she was challenging me to be a leader, to be better than I was acting, and she didn't have to say a word. She didn't know American Sign Language, but when I wanted to go run off with the older kids, she knew how to point at me and communicate that I was staying there with her. All that love, creativity, and wisdom are what I hold in my heart.

Maybe some people might have judged my Aunt Bett based on their perceptions of her abilities as a person who was deaf and mute. We do that to each other too much, you know? Judging folks. Putting limitations on them. But those same people missed out on so much. My Aunt Bett lived a full life and left a legacy of wisdom that I will forever carry with me.

26

GET IT CLEAN

"You can fall, but you can rise also."

—ANGÉLIQUE KIDJO

In our house, and probably in many households in the South, the rule was that Saturday was cleanup day. The morning was set aside for cleaning the whole house. In our home, everyone had different responsibilities. My job was dusting, and it included dusting my mama's bell collection. She had 237 bells. I know that, honey, because I had to count them every doggone week.

One particular Saturday, I didn't pick up the bells. I used the little duster to just wipe around them. Usually, I'd dust and wipe the inside of the bell as well as the shelf where it sat. But on this sunny North Carolina weekend, I wanted to go outside and play. By just doing a quick dust on the outside of the bell, I got finished quicker. Then I went to my room and rushed through cleaning it. I pushed stuff under my bed and shoved everything else in my closet, closing my door. From just the naked eye, at first glance, my room looked clean. The bells looked dusted. The tables looked clean. I was good, right?

I thought so. Honey, I threw on my play clothes and outside I went. I was out there just having me a good ol' time.

We had a carport with a deck connected to it, and my daddy had a way of stepping out there and yelling my name. The wind seemed to carry Daddy's voice so clearly. When my daddy called my name, everybody within earshot said, "Oh . . ." If things were fine and he just needed me for something, he'd say, "Tabitha!" But baby, if he said my middle name, too, I knew something wrong. That day, I heard my daddy yell, "Tabitha Bonita!"

I was in the circular street with my neighbor on a little skateboard going up and down the little hill near the house. As soon as I heard Daddy, I said, "Uh-oh."

That walk home was so doggone long. Well, not that walk—that *run*. It might have felt like I was walking because I was so nervous, but honey, I ran home.

"Yes, sir. Daddy?"

My mom and dad were standing in our living room. Moma said, "What's your job in here? What's your responsibility?"

I said, "To clean and dust the bells. To dust the tables and stuff."

"Well, pick that bell up right there."

She pointed to the silver-painted cowbell, one of my favorites. When I picked it up, you could see the circle of dust
on the table, a perfect ring. They both looked at me and said
some version of "What is that?"

I said, "Dust."

Then Moma said, "Pick up another bell. Pick up another
one."

I picked up three or four bells, and all you could see were
these circles in the dust on the table.

"I thought you dusted?"

"I did."

Moma said, "No, you took a shortcut. You didn't want to
do the full job. You dusted around the bells, and you dusted
on top of them. But you see how we knew what you did? All
we did was pick it up to see the evidence that you didn't do
it right."

All I could manage was, "Yes, ma'am. Yes, sir."

Then my dad said, "Come up here to this room." I walked
up the steps behind him to my bedroom. He lifted up my
little twin bed and under it was all my little toys, some
shoes and clothes. Everything I had stuffed under there.
Daddy said, "Now, why did you do that?"

"Because I wanted to go outside and play."

"So you were in such a rush that you just stuffed all that
under there and didn't do what you were told. You tried to
trick us and make us think you had cleaned your room, but
all you really did was straighten up."

That's when they both sat me down and had a conversation. "There's a difference between straightening up and

cleaning up. When you clean up, you clean under that bed. You pick up those bells and you dust them. That way, when we come back around and check your work, there's nothing to be found. Because you did what you were supposed to do."

My mom used to tell me, "Look, when you have company coming over to the house, you can't just straighten up the house. You got to clean up."

I'm sure I gave her the classic nine-year-old blank stare.

Nevertheless, she continued, "Because if you just straighten up, that means if somebody sits on the couch, they might be able to look under the chair and see all the dust and socks and different things you missed. Do you want somebody to sit on your bed and find a nasty pair of drawers up under your chair? You don't want to be embarrassed about that." She then would give me a tutorial on what it meant to clean the house as opposed to just straightening it up.

Lift up the chairs.

Lift the couches.

Lift up your bed.

Clean everything from under all those places.

Put everything away.

Wash, fold, and put away your clothes.

Vacuum the carpets.

Mop the floors.

Pick up each bell.

Moma taught me that you should never have to worry about being embarrassed about what guests may find when they come over if you truly clean up.

At such a young age, I honestly thought their lessons were just about cleaning up the house. But as I became an adult, I realized that this same principle could be applied to the way we approach our lives.

If you simply just straighten up your life, you still leave room for people to pull back the covers and see everything that you didn't actually fix. You still leave room for people to see your wrongs, flaws, and dirt. But if you clean up your life, they can search, and search, and search, and they won't find anything but you.

Some of us have just been straightening up our lives. We haven't decided to clean it up yet. There's a huge difference, honey. If you just do the bare minimum so you look good on the surface, folks who come into your life may find out or see some things you didn't want them to see. Your life might look good on the outside, but if somebody looks really closely, they will see what you've been hiding.

We've seen the straightened-up folks. We've *been* the straightened-up folks. It's like being in a rush to go somewhere and not having time to take a bath. You change your clothes. Put on some perfume or cologne. You may look good. Maybe even smell alright from a distance. But honey, God forbid somebody gets too close. Then they see the ring around the top of your shirt. Or they find out them drawers are dirty. Whew!

If you clean up your life, baby, they (or you!) can look all they want to, but they won't find a thing. And honestly, it isn't even about what *other* people uncover in your "dirty house." Honey, *you* will feel better when your life is clean.

Now, listen, I'm not pointing any fingers. We all must check ourselves. There's an old song I used to hear growing up. The Canton Spirituals used to sing, "I've got to clean up . . . what I messed up." We all have to do that sometimes, right? Let's commit to asking ourselves on a regular basis, *Am I straightening up or cleaning up?*

Which way do you want to live? I prefer to live a clean life, with no hidden dirt. It makes the blessings come easier.

And honey, don't just straighten up your life and then invite somebody into it thinking they ain't going to catch nothing. People *will* notice. *You* will notice. Take your time and really clean it up. Be ready for anybody or anything to come into your life because you know it's clean. You ain't got nothing to hide. And even if they bring up something from your past, if you've cleaned up, it won't matter. You'll be ready to have a conversation about it because you know it's not still hiding underneath the perfect picture you think you've painted.

Yes, cleaning up our lives means we have to face all that dirty stuff. All those things that have piled up in our hearts and minds. That can be uncomfortable, for sure. When my daddy lifted up my mattress and saw everything I tucked down under there, I felt exposed. Uncomfortable. It's such a terrible feeling to have trouble pending because you didn't take care of your dirt. But my parents blessed me with the best lesson I've ever learned in my life. If you are really ready to take on life, to take on anything or anybody that comes your way, clean that thing up, no matter what *it* is. You know where the dirt is. It could be major or minor. Whatever it is, it's yours, and that's your business. But don't just straighten it up—make sure you clean it up.

YOU'RE ALRIGHT

"The kind of beauty I want most is the
hard-to-get kind that comes from within—
strength, courage, dignity."

—RUBY DEE

We all change.

Do you hear me?

We all look different than we used to, whether that's better or, in our minds, worse. It doesn't mean our souls—who we are on the inside—are any better or worse. It's simply a change in appearance.

Too many of us, when we hear phrases like "forever young," we think our bodies are supposed to feel the way they felt twenty or thirty years ago. But when I think about that statement, I think of our spiritual selves. Our spirits can always feel forever young and vibrant, but our bodies were created to age and grow.

As we get older, new pains will come. Sometimes we don't have to do anything but get up out of the bed and we're saying, "Lord Jesus, my leg is hurting." That's been me many times. We have these steps in our new home and my legs are like, "Ooh, girl. You going up and down stairs now? This is what we're doing now?"

But even when we feel those little aches and pains, let's try to use them as a reminder that we are alive. That we are growing.

I learned a thing or two about this from the elderly patients at the assisted living home I worked at years ago. There was this one woman, Miriam, who was celebrating her ninety-sixth birthday. I jokingly said, "Honey, how old are you? Twenty-five?"

She said to me, "I'm ninety-six."

"What?! You're ninety-six? There ain't no way, girl. You look about thirty years old."

I'm joking around with her, thinking I'm making her feel good. Honey, guess what she said?

"You know what? I'm excited about being ninety-six, because that means I got old. And if you don't get old, that means you must have died young."

Baby, that thing hit me like a ton of bricks. I said, "Wait a minute, now, Miriam. You're preaching, girl."

I was so overwhelmed. All I could think about was my mother, who died at fifty-one. By the time she passed away, she couldn't move anything in her body other than her eyes and a little bit of her lips. She was completely bedridden and paralyzed because of ALS. All Moma wanted to do was to be able to move and get up out of that bed. She died feeling every change in her body. She died young.

So when Miriam said that, it was a wake-up call. I decided to embrace every single change and every single year I'm given. I don't want to be the same as I was at twenty-one. That Tab didn't know what Tab knows now. I was taking diet pills at twenty-one. The box suggested taking two a day? Well, I would take four or six to try to speed up the process. Same thing with laxatives. Twenty-one-year-old to thirty-one-year-old Tab was weighing herself a million times a day. In my forties now, I have more knowledge. I'm wiser and smarter now. My mind is sharper. My heart is kinder; I'm more loving to myself. I'm more patient now. Honey, I am grateful for the little extra cushion on my body, too. Got me a couple extra curves, and I ain't mad about them. But I'm a grown woman and I know that I'm enough just as I am. Bottom line? I've grown. And I suspect that as I get older, God willing, I'll grow even more.

I prefer all of that over any thin or so-called perfect body any day. Yes, I work out. I try my best to be healthy and look good in my clothes. But my intention is always to better myself inside and out.

Baby, I know what it is to gain weight and get sick and have to wrestle with my change in appearance. Your face looks different. Maybe your body is different. It doesn't feel the same. Maybe you don't feel as pretty or as handsome as you once felt. But honey, you are still you. This body is nothing but a shell. Our flesh is not the same as our spirit. Yes, there may be some things that link the two. Sometimes the state of our spirits is reflected in our bodies. But the way you deal with that kind of change is not to wallow in the outer changes. Focus on the inner work you have to do, because when that is beautiful, it doesn't matter much what happens on the outside. In fact, the outside will probably go the way of the inside, okay?

Yes, you might be going through some things that have changed your physical body drastically. Maybe illness has your body not functioning at its best. Lord knows, I know how that feels. But be mindful to not allow the state of your body to impact the state of your spirit. Shore up your mind, strengthen your spirit—in whatever ways are best for you.

Stay mentally and spiritually sound. Because the moment you allow the way your body feels to influence how your mind and heart feel, you've lost. My mom taught me that when she was first diagnosed. They gave her six to eight months to live. She lived for three years, because although her body was failing her, she never believed in her sickness. She would always think positive, and when the doctors would say one thing, she would remind us all that God had the final say, and He hadn't told her what the doctor was saying about the time she had left!

However, I've been on the other end of that mind-versus-body fight, and for a while, I was losing. I've dealt with depression and had major anxiety attacks. I've been on medication—steroids, in particular—that caused me to gain weight and feel terrible. I didn't want to get out of the bed. In fact, I looked for any reason just to sleep. So I get it. It's hard to navigate a tough season of physical and mental pain. But honey, I believe your situation is temporary. Even if it's not physically short-lived, you can strengthen how your mind and soul process what you're going through. You are worthy. Period. No matter what. And the more you understand how worthy you are, the more likely you'll find your strength again. You've got to believe that! Say to yourself, *This is temporary. I'm going to get through this.*

Fight against those feelings of wanting to give up; of not being worthy of feeling better. Don't lie down. Rest, but then get up on the days you can and fight for what you deserve. Honey, you are worthy of feeling better, doing better, and being better. Keep working on your mind and heart. I don't care what the outside looks like. You are beautiful. Once you find your inner peace and beauty, you'll never let yourself go. Even if it feels like your body is failing you, focus on what is true on the inside. Be present, and everything else, honey, will pass.

One day you will look in the mirror and say, *Oh, I'm alright.* That's the goal, honey. To look in the mirror and be okay with whatever you see looking back. Continue to work on yourself. Do as much as you can. Get up and do something amazing for you. Maybe try something you've never done before. But don't let your situation now determine how you will live your life forever.

Let's embrace all our new journeys. Let's not focus on what we used to be, but who we are right now and can be in the future. Change is good. Matter of fact, change is a great thing. So let's embrace the changes—good and bad—our bodies go through. Let's embrace all our feelings, the life we live, and our current situations. We're supposed to change. We are forever evolving, and that's okay. Change means we're still growing and we're still alive to do so.

Very good.

28

PERMANENT LESSONS FROM YOUR TEMPORARY SEASON

"Opportunity often comes disguised in the form of misfortune or temporary defeat."

—NAPOLEON HILL

I've had so many different jobs in my life. And I've always believed that we are often put in a place for a reason— even if we are only there for a season. For me, it's usually in hindsight when I look back at jobs I've had and realize, *Oh, that's why I was there!*

For five years, I worked for a company called APAC, which served as the call center for UPS customer service. At a very young age, barely twenty-one, I became a supervisor in charge of about fifty people, all of whom were older than me. Some were even my parents' age. That position taught me how to stand in my power. Of course, at the time, I did not realize that it was building me. I was just doing my work and making sure I did it well. I enjoyed my job because I loved helping and guiding people.

Now I realize that this position taught me that every person has a story. I used to do one-on-one sessions with the employees I was responsible for supervising. If someone called in their shift, I'd have to sit down and talk with them—sometimes even write them up—but in the process they'd give their reasons for why they called in. Many times people were going through things, and I think that job helped teach me empathy. Of course, I didn't believe everything I was told, because I knew that not everybody was always telling the truth. But there were times when I really had to ask myself, *What if it was me? What if my child was sick, or what if it was my mother, or my father who was sick?* Because life was happening to these people, just as it was happening to me.

Yes, the corporate rules were very strict, but I was also in charge. So I learned that sometimes it's okay to give a little bit. That job was my intro class in learning how to practice patience and understanding with people, something I do today.

A more practical lesson I learned from working for UPS

was the ins and outs of shipping. Not much has changed since my days there. I know how to run the logistics side of my business because I worked there. I know how to make sure I get things shipped out in a timely manner. I know how to pack and measure. I know how to make customs slips and ship international.

The call center supervisor job also served as a stepping-stone. The training and experience I already had helped me get the nine-to-five jobs I needed when I arrived in LA. Back when I was twenty, I remember complaining that the training was so hard. "Oh my God, this is too much," I'd say. Honey, me and my husband, who also worked there, would call it boot camp. But we now say, "You know what? That job prepared us for every other job we've ever had." Simply *because* it was so hard. It was so thorough. You had to cross every *t* and dot every *i*. I really appreciated every job that came after it, because with each new opportunity, I realized just how much that training had prepared me.

That said, there were certainly times when I would feel stuck and think, *Is this going to be my whole life? Am I going to be here forever?* But I was so grateful that God had my ear. He'd told me, *This is not the life I planned for you.* I'd been working. I still intended to return to LA, to my dream. But Chance was concerned that we needed more money.

This is not the life I planned for you.

I walked into my job at APAC not too long after talking to Chance about moving back to LA, and they had begun laying people off. Many of the new customer service reps, and even some who'd been there for a long time and were making more money, were being laid off. Because I'd taken the time to get to know them and their stories, I knew they needed their jobs. For many of them, this *was* going to be their lives, and that was okay. They were going to stay there for as long as they could. Some would even retire from there. But that wasn't my story. I knew it was a temporary season for me. So one morning, I told my husband, "I'm going to go in there and volunteer to be laid off so that I can spare two of my reps. I make double what they make, so that means two of them can keep their job."

Honey, I walked down the hallway that morning and felt like I was floating. I was so excited because I knew I was about to take a leap. I knew that my decision was going to start something new inside me. I felt a confirmation in my spirit that day and knew that nothing could stop me. Chance was on board, and I was feeling like, *It's going down today.*

And that's exactly what I did. I went into human resources and said, "Listen, I will take a layoff, but please keep two of my reps that you were going to lay off. Let them keep their jobs." They said yes and gave me a severance package. That same severance package was the money that helped us move to LA in 2004.

This is not the life I planned for you.

Years later, I was a certified nursing assistant at the assisted-living home in Palmdale, California. I worked the night shift, and there were so many nights that I cried. I would go in the bathroom and just look at myself in the mirror and say, "Girl, what are you doing? How did we get here?" But once again, I had to remind myself that it was temporary. God had put something in my spirit; in my heart, mind, and dreams. That job was simply going to pay us in the meantime. At the time, I didn't know how long I was going to be doing it. But I trusted that there was something else waiting for me. I knew what God told me. These jobs were part of the plan, but they weren't *the* plan. Greater was coming.

I think we all have to do that. We have to constantly remind ourselves of our dreams. When we're not living in our purpose, we have to remind ourselves that the situation we're in has to be temporary because our dreams are real. They are possible. The desires of my heart will come to pass because God has a plan for me. We have to keep telling ourselves that we are going to get through it. We have to keep going.

I know how it feels to feel stuck. It's uncomfortable. But there's also a discomfort that comes when God has been trying to move you and you won't move. He'll make you uncomfortable until you get forced to move. He did that to me many times as well. Don't wait until things get so bad that God has to make you so uncomfortable just to push you out of your comfort zone. Take those steps yourself. Be ready to take your leaps of faith. Trust yourself. Trust that gut, that feeling deep down on the inside. It's there. That's our gift. And remember, wherever you are, it's only temporary.

VEGAN FISH STICKS

Remember when we were kids and fish sticks were everything? Not only do fish sticks take me back to my childhood, they're also one of my husband's favorite things. When I figured out I could use hearts of palm to make a vegan fish stick, baby, the inner child in me said, "Oh, God, we thank you." Let's make some.

A little bit of fish fry (seafood breading mix)

Some chickpea (garbanzo bean) flour *(although any flour will do)*

Old Bay seasoning

Dill (fresh or dried)

A multi-spice seasoning blend *(McCormick makes a salt-free one I really love, with garlic, onion, paprika, black pepper, celery, and turmeric powder)*

A little furikake *(it's what's going to give you that fish flavor)*

Some nondairy milk *(Tab loves unsweetened cashew milk)*

A can of hearts of palm *(get the whole kind or the ones sliced lengthwise; try to avoid the salad-cut version)*

Grapeseed oil, for frying

Tartar sauce

Vegan mayo

Dill *(a little or a lot, fresh or not—that's your business)*

Garlic powder

Sweet relish

Chile paste

We're going to make two mixtures, one wet and one dry.

To create your dry mixture, in a bowl, add 1½ cups fish fry, 1½ cups chickpea flour, Old Bay, a sprinkle of dill, the seasoning blend, and the furikake.

To create your wet mixture, put half the dry mix in a separate bowl. Add the milk—enough to make it thick but not lumpy. If it's too thin, use a little extra—and stir until the batter is smooth.

Pour some oil into a frying pan—enough that it'll mostly cover the hearts of palm once you've added them. And be sure the pan is tall enough that the oil can't escape! Heat the oil to 400°F.

Now, usually hearts of palm come in thick, long pieces. We're going to rinse those off and dip them directly into the wet mix. Keep your dry mix close by, because you'll need it soon. Roll the hearts of palm around really good in the wet mix so they are completely coated.

Then dip your hearts of palm in your dry mix, okay?

If you want to do a double coat—wet and dry again—go right ahead. That's your business. But you don't have to.

Once the hearts of palm are completely coated, drop them into the hot oil to fry, and if they aren't covered in the oil, turn them as they cook until all sides are golden brown. (Turn gently so as not to disturb the delicious crust.) When you take them out, put them on a paper towel and let them drain a little bit.

This is a comfort food, okay? Fried fish sticks. Thank you, God!

Oh, wait a minute! I can't forget the tartar sauce. Grab you some vegan mayo, some dill, and some garlic powder. Mix that together and then add some sweet relish and, if you like some kick, a little chile paste. Mix it together, and now you have your tartar.

CREATE YOUR VILLAGE

*"In every conceivable manner, the family is
a link to our past, a bridge to our future."*

—ALEX HALEY

Family is everything to me. Like my dad taught me early on, it is the foundation of everything you do. It's just like building a house. If you construct a home with no foundation, it's going to fall every time. But if you have a foundation, a storm could come blow your whole house over and the foundation will still be there. You could rebuild the home exactly as it was—or even better.

I learned about the power of strong family bonds when my mom was sick. I shared with you already our journey in navigating our feelings about how to take care of my mother. That experience taught me so much about patience and expectations and how to love no matter what. But there is another part of this experience that is just as important.

Sometimes, we have to create our own family.

When I was traveling back and forth from California to North Carolina to care for my mama, Chance stayed in California with our baby girl. Our created family was a huge support system during that time. While I was away, this extension of our family, this village, was there to help my husband take care of our daughter.

Having a village outside your immediate family is so important, because you never know when life will take an unexpected turn. But if you have this village, if you have the support of both family and friends, you can trust that you have something holding you in place when the storms come.

Their actions—whether it's babysitting or lending money or something else—certainly help things run a little bit more smoothly. But their love will hold you up when you are feeling the weight of whatever loss or grief you're experiencing.

I'm writing this book in the midst of a global pandemic. COVID-19 has created so much havoc and chaos in our lives, with seemingly no end in sight. But even then, having a support system, someone to call on, can make all the difference in whether the isolation gets the best of us or not. My daddy is my best friend. Because he lives three thousand miles away, I don't get to see him very often. The pandemic has now made traveling as freely as I might have in the past out of the question, so those daily phone and FaceTime calls are everything. I look forward to those little nuggets of wisdom he gives me. It's like a lifeline.

Having blood family as a support system is such a blessing. Even with me pursuing my career, my cousins, aunts, and uncles have always been very supportive and encouraging. I'm sure they thought I was crazy with all my dreams and whatnot, but they still cheered me on. But I also understand that not everyone is blessed with that blood family who can hold them up in that way. So as you go on your life journey, be discerning about the people in your life who could potentially be part of your village. Don't be afraid to make your own family.

Life could have been more difficult without our LA family. It's hard for me to even call them friends, because they are really like brothers and sisters to me. My kids refer to them as aunts and uncles. Whether blood or found family, sometimes you need to know that you have somebody who's going to have your back if anything goes down. Knowing you have that is so healing to the soul.

I used to host dinners at my house every Sunday. It didn't matter if we were in our little Baldwin Hills apartment or one of the two houses we eventually moved to—I'd bring my Southern flavor and hospitality and throw down on a big meal for our found family. This was BV (Before Vegan), so you were likely to find all kinds of down-home soul food on the table.

This was even more important to me because, as an actor,

I'd run into all kinds of people at classes or in workshops who didn't have any family in LA. They'd come here, just like I did, to pursue a dream. I wanted them to feel like my husband, daughter, and me were their family, so I'd say, "Y'all come over Sunday. I'm cooking!" And they came! Some people would bring their own dishes, and we'd have a wonderful time. This is how we created family, and it was a beautiful thing. Many of those same people who started coming to my Sunday dinners fifteen or sixteen years ago still come to my house right now, although not every Sunday these days, to eat all my vegan goodies.

The village my husband and I created has been the most powerful representation of love and care I've seen. It's hard to be somewhere knowing that your blood family is all the way across the country. And meeting new people can be intimidating. But, if you're open to it, if you're open to what can come from those new relationships, it is so rewarding.

I know so many families like mine who had one person who sort of kept everything and everyone together. For me, it was my grandma Etta. Grandma Etta, my father's mother, had twelve kids and kept up with everyone. Ten out of those twelve children had their own children, and their children had children, yet somehow Grandma Etta managed to make you feel like you were her only one. She was connected with each of us in her own special way.

Every Sunday, we had what felt like a family reunion at Grandma Etta's house. After church, we all got together and ate dinner and fellowshipped with each other. This is where we all caught up on what everyone was doing or what someone needed. The family was very close, and still is. My grandmother has been gone now for twenty years, but though she has passed away, my family still continues to spend holidays together. They do Sundays once a month. And even though I live all the way out in Los Angeles and don't get to participate much, it does my heart good to know that the family is still connecting with each other in that way. They still have that day where they say, "We're going over this cousin's house or that cousin's house." Everyone continues to stick together, just like when my grandma was alive.

But for some people, when a matriarch or patriarch passes away, the family begins to fracture. Their death causes separation in the family and allows for old hurts and unresolved secrets to come to the surface and cause problems.

Honey, it shouldn't be that way. We have to try to make things right within our families. Our grandparents, mothers, and fathers often do a phenomenal job in holding us together. But when God calls them home, that doesn't mean the family should be scattered and divided. We are supposed to try to do our best to stick together and love each other, just like they taught us.

Maybe your mother or father has passed and you haven't talked to your sister or brother since the funeral. Or maybe your grandmother is gone, and the cousins haven't kept in touch. Maybe there was some confusion or frustration over a will or inheritance. Nothing is worth separating yourself from the love of your family, baby. Family is so important. Having a village to support and hold you up is critical. Yes, you might have to create your own village for any number of reasons. But if you have blood family and you know you all can work things out, then take the step to do just that. Nobody's family is perfect. Everybody has problems. But they are still your family and it's worth trying. Ask yourself, *Why haven't I talked to my sister? Why don't I know what's going on with my brother? Why doesn't my family get together anymore? Why don't we even call and check in on each other?* Now, by no means am I saying to let anyone hurt you with toxicity, but if you feel it's a situation that can be healed, try to make it right.

I know. Life is happening at lightning speed right now. We all got a lot going on. But if you are intentionally trying not to see your family, unpack the reason for that. Make sure you're clear. What are you mad about? You know good and well that your grandmama or mama or daddy or whoever was the glue for your family would be upset if they knew that the family wasn't taking care of each other.

Let's get back to loving each other. Not from a distance. I mean up close. Let's go see each other. Check on each other. Sometimes I think that's all we need. Let's tap into the spirits of our grandmas and great-grandmas, our granddaddies, aunts, and uncles. It feels good when you have family, and it feels even better when you're together. There's somebody out there who doesn't have family. Who has to create one, not because they are far away like me, but because they literally don't have anyone left. They are wishing they had someone they could call. So think about that, alright? Even if they cut up and act a fool sometimes, they are still your family, and you are a part of them. Go fix that thing.

30

THERE'S ALWAYS A WAY

*"When you know your name, you should
hang on to it, for unless it is noted down
and remembered, it will die when you do."*

—TONI MORRISON, *SONG OF SOLOMON*

My mother passed away of the neuromuscular disease
ALS, also called Lou Gehrig's disease. If you're not
familiar with ALS, let's just say it's a rare condition that
comes out of nowhere. It's not particular at all about who it
chooses, and it can strike anybody. My mother was a social
worker and, later on in her life, a pastor. But everything
shifted dramatically in the years between her diagnosis and
her transition.

The disease usually starts in a limb. It attacks your muscles, putting them to sleep. When that happens, your brain

can't get the message to them to do whatever they need to do. So if it starts in your foot, you'll lose your ability to walk. From there, the illness spreads and eventually captures the organs.

With Moma, it started in her hands. She knew something was not right. Her right hand would get weak and twitch, and she couldn't use it anymore. It just wouldn't move. Months later, it went to her right foot, and then the entire right side of her body. But here's part of why I'm sharing this with you: When my mom, who was working on a memoir at the time, lost the use of her writing hand, she didn't put her pen down. In a matter of weeks, she taught herself to write with her left hand. When she could no longer write at all, she asked us to get her a tape recorder because she was still able to talk and so she wanted to record herself.

My mother was determined to write her story. She was dedicated to the process of getting it all out. And it didn't matter that her body was shutting down on her; she was going to make a way. She would always say, "I can't die with this stuff inside me. It needs to live long after I'm gone." I got my persistence honestly.

A few days before Moma passed, she mouthed to me—she couldn't talk any longer, so we'd read her lips—that she wanted me to be sure to get the box. "The box" was filled with all her tapes and journals—everything she wanted to share. I did what she asked, and I still have that box to this day. But a week after my mom passed, I tried to listen to one of the tapes, and I couldn't. I suppose it was too soon. I even tried to read some of her journals early on, and it was all a bit too much at the time.

It took me nearly twelve years to open that box again.

I had an urge to listen and was at a point in my life when I wasn't going to ignore those urges. The first problem I faced, though, was the tapes. By then, nobody was walking around with a tape player. But I eventually found a cassette player and decided to revisit with a listen.

Three minutes into the first tape and I shut it off quickly. My mother was praying. Her voice was sweet but powerful. It was like music to my ears. But I hadn't heard it in more than twelve years. She had such a delicate tone. A true lady, in every way. I fell into tears because I missed her, yes, but also because I was thankful that she took the time, made a way out of no way, to leave her voice with me. It didn't matter if she had to poke the record button with a pencil she'd picked up with her mouth; she persisted.

I turned the tape player back on and listened to my mother praying and giving praise. It was clear that she was in a state of gratitude. She knew she was going to die. She'd been given the prognosis and told, "You are sick. There's nothing we can do to make you better. This disease is terminal." Yet she was thankful. She started listing the things she was grateful for, and one of them was the fact that she'd just left California. This was not long after Chance and I had moved to LA.

"Well, I got to go to California, stay with my baby daughter, Tabitha, my son-in-law, Chance, and my grandbaby,

Choyce. I had to get out there because I got to see where my baby is going to be. I got to see where she's going to be at, because the Lord has called her out there for something."

Out of the piles and piles of cassette tapes I could have chosen to listen to, I picked that one up. God is always on the job, that's for sure.

She went on to talk about the pain she was enduring emotionally with my stepfather. As I shared earlier, he wasn't dealing with her illness well. He couldn't handle it, and because of that anger, he became distant and unlike himself. But even still, despite living with that, she expressed her gratitude. The posture of her heart until the day she took her last breath was thankfulness.

Listen, nobody wants to get sick. Nobody wants to have to rely on someone else to take care of their basic needs. And it can certainly be frustrating for caregivers. But be kind. People are just happy to be alive. Our kindness fuels their gratitude, and hopefully our own. Instead of allowing grief and anger to have the last say, enjoy those last days, months, or years with your loved one. Spend that time with them.

I think Moma was determined to tell her story because she knew something I didn't at the time. Despite knowing she was going to die, she used to say, "Girl, people going to know my name!"

"Well, Moma, I believe so," I'd respond.

"Because you're going to see to it," she'd say back to me.

I didn't get it at that time. I couldn't catch the prophecy in her words. But now I know what she was saying.

My mama's name is Patricia Blackstock Johnson. She was amazing and strong.

Baby, when everything and everyone is telling you that you can't do something, there's still a way. When you feel like you've tried everything, there's still a way. When you get to that crossroads and start feeling like you can do it, but you can't figure out what's next, I want you to whisper this to yourself: *Patricia Blackstock Johnson*. I want you to remember that if Tab's mama can put a pencil in her mouth to hit record on her tape recorder, what can you not do? Where there's a will, there's a way. All you have to do is have the willpower to keep going. Even when it looks like it's going to be over or the storm is too powerful, honey, stay in a state of gratitude. Give God praise in advance.

When my mama left this world, she was at peace. I'd never seen a person so at peace in my life. She'd told us the day she was going home, and she was at peace about it. She was right. People do know her name. You know her name. Her name is now a mantra and a scripture in the mouths of so many who are going to choose not to let their spirits be troubled, who are going to choose gratitude and peace. And for that alone, I give thanks! Thanks, Moma.

A FINAL TSA

 So you've done the work, right? You've left the negative mind-set behind. You've even let go of some people who didn't have your best interests at heart. You're pressing toward your dreams and working while you're waiting for them to come true. You've got your village in place. And maybe things are starting to happen for you. I'm so happy for you. I really am. But there's one more thing: God didn't take you on that journey so you can keep it to yourself. You didn't go through those ups and downs so you can just sit on it and not share it to help someone else. That ain't the point of living.

I know that part of the purpose God has given me is to help save lives. That's my assignment. I want to do that by helping folks eat healthier and be kind to themselves and others. We've got to do better by our bodies, baby. And Tab is called to do that work. But if in the process of doing that, my life starts to change—just as it has—and I don't tell you how I got here? Well, then I'm not doing right by my assignment. I'll go as far as to say I would be a hypocrite.

God is still in the healing business. I know it's easy to think that God isn't healing the way it says He did in the Bible or other sacred texts. But listen, God is the same yesterday, today, and tomorrow. I remember one day back when I first started doing videos, I heard in my spirit a message that I couldn't let go. God didn't want me to write it in a Facebook post. He didn't want me to wait and deliver it some other way. He wanted me to go live right that instant, and so I did. In that message I shared my story of God healing me after a year and seven months of pain. I talked about how I'd prayed to God for healing and committed to submitting my life to Him if He did. I stood there in front of however many thousands of people who had logged in and testified about the healing power of God.

I don't know why there was such an urgency. Or why I felt like I had to go live right then. But it was my business to be obedient to the feeling and spirit. I do believe that there was probably someone—or even several someones—who needed to hear my voice in that moment. They needed to know that despite chronic pain and sickness, they could be healed. Despite doctors not being able to figure out what was wrong or not having a clue how to proceed, God still heals. And yes, my story has to do with health, but there were probably a few folks who needed healing in their relationships or in their finances. They needed me to share my story and say over and over again, "God is still in the healing business." They needed to know that their situation, whatever it was, didn't catch God off guard. It wasn't new to Him. They might have been tired and thought they were just going to log on to get a few recipes or laugh with Tab about something crazy happening with my family. But God met them through my story.

Surrender your need to be in charge of your story. Somebody is waiting to receive God's healing through your words. Swallow that pride. Love yourself and others enough to share what God is doing.

We must share the ways God's grace, mercy, and blessings

show up in our lives. That's the mandate after we reach our goals. After you stand in that mirror and speak life to yourself, go on ahead and speak life to someone else.

The shift is happening for you. I know you feel it. You might not know that change is on the horizon. You might just feel awfully uncomfortable, or you may feel unexplainably excited! *That's the shift.* You've gotten in the car, stepped on the gas, and put everything in gear. Now God is showing out. You are entering your winning season, and I'm cheering for you. So then, why in the world would you not share that with someone? There's someone watching you right now who is scared; they don't even want to get in the car. They are overwhelmed by life just like you were a short time ago. Go bless them with your story. Pay the love forward. That's what we're here to do. And if you're still scared and feeling stuck, remember this season is temporary and it will pass! Hang on in there and keep on going! I love you!

ACKNOWLEDGMENTS

First and foremost, I just have to thank God for this moment. It feels surreal. I can't believe He has placed me on this journey, but I'm so grateful He has. Everything He took me through was for this day and this book. I'm so forever thankful.

Thank you to my husband, Chance, who has been right by my side through thick and thin, honey. Through good and bad, in sickness and in health, you have stayed by my side through it all. Now here we are, able to reap the benefits and rewards of never giving up on each other and you never giving up on me. Thank you, Chance. I love you, babe.

To my children, Choyce, Queston, and Ty-Leah: Every day, you make me a better woman, a better mom, and a better person. I pray every day that Mommy inspires you to grow up and be even better than I am. May your dreams be bigger than mine, and your lives full of abundant blessings. I love you all.

To my sister, Tasha, who is my right hand when my left is preoccupied, who does everything that I ever ask, I thank you. I love you for loving me and for just always being there.

To my stepmom, Diane, I thank you for loving me as your own. I appreciate you.

To Moma: I know that my strength comes from you. I know that the experience of your life helped shape my life today. I thank God for you, and I thank Him for choosing me to be your child. I will continue to carry the torch that you lit first. I miss you and love you, Moma.

To Daddy: I'm so very thankful that you are not only my daddy, but my best friend. The one who has always been an open ear for me. But more than that, you have always been my encourager, my pusher, the one who said, "I don't know how to get you to them dreams you got, but we're going to help you and we're going to try and I'm going to always support you." You are my everything, Daddy. Thank you and I love you.

To my team: Kyle Santillo and Clayton Santillo at Scale Management; Cindy Uh and Carlos Segarra at Creative Artists Agency; and my editor, Cassie Jones, and the whole William Morrow team at HarperCollins. Thank you all so very much for believing in me, for trusting me, and for confirming that I am enough. Thank you for flying with me. I love you all. God bless you.

To Tracey Michae'l Lewis-Giggetts: I cannot even thank you enough. I absolutely love you. I appreciate you for all the long days and nights of writing with and for me; for messaging me and letting me talk on voice recordings. For not just hearing me, but actually capturing my voice and making sure it never fell short. I thank you, sister, for that. And I look forward to many more to come. God bless you. I love you.

Now . . . let's get to feeding the soul!